Kaufman

T0309845

Andy Kaufman

Wrestling with the American Dream

Florian Keller

University of Minnesota Press
Minneapolis • London

Published by the University of Minnesota Press
111 Third Avenue South, Suite 290
Minneapolis, MN 55401-2520
http://www.upress.umn.edu

Printed in the United States of America on acid-free paper

Library of Congress Cataloging-in-Publication Data

Keller, Florian.
   Andy Kaufman : wrestling with the American dream / Florian Keller.
      p. cm.
   Filmography: p.
   Includes bibliographical references and index.
   ISBN 0-8166-4602-3 (hc : alk. paper) — ISBN 0-8166-4603-1 (pb : alk.
paper) 1. Kaufman, Andy, 1949-1984. I. Title.
   PN2287.K28K45 2005
   792.702´8´092—dc22

                                                       2005020437

The University of Minnesota is an equal-opportunity educator and employer.

12 11 10 09 08 07 06 05   10 9 8 7 6 5 4 3 2 1

Contents

Preface

This is not a book about comedy. Though it deals with one of the most puzzling performers to emerge from American stand-up comedy in the past three decades, this is not a study about how Andy Kaufman may have transcended, or undermined, the rhetoric of comedy. Rather, what I offer is an analysis of the American social imaginary, based on Andy Kaufman as the artist who enacted America's collective fantasies in such a way as to render visible the contradictions that haunt these fantasies.

An enigmatic entertainer who was often endearing, disturbing, and annoying at the same time, Andy Kaufman (born 1949) is widely recognized as one of the seminal artists in the history of American pop culture. He was one of the most controversial American entertainers, and his performance work was too bizarre to be easily labeled as comedy. Foreign Man, the most lovable of his personae, usually acted like a complete failure in terms of traditional stand-up comedy, but when this incompetent joker morphed into a copy of Elvis Presley, Kaufman's impression was breathtaking. When Foreign Man was cast as a character for the television sitcom *Taxi*, an obscene lounge singer by the name of Tony Clifton caused mayhem on the set. Tony Clifton, of course, was Andy Kaufman, though he was not. After all, Kaufman was innocuous Uncle Andy, who would involve his audience in infantile sing-along acts. Kaufman was this nice entertainer who invited his entire audience at Carnegie Hall for a midnight snack of milk and cookies in the cafeteria at the New York School of Printing.

Around the time when Milos Forman's Hollywood biopic *Man on the Moon* (1999) was released, popular interest in Kaufman reached its peak, but as far as serious cultural analysis is concerned, his work has remained largely uncharted territory since his untimely death from lung cancer in 1984. Ever since his first stage acts, Kaufman's performances often prompted comparisons with avant-gardists like Ionesco, Pirandello, or Duchamp; this book is the first effort to read his work not in terms of any kind of (European) avant-garde but specifically within the context of American culture. Taking *Man on the Moon* as my starting point, I argue that the irritation Kaufman provoked had nothing to do with the way he stretched the formal conventions of comedy but instead was a result of his persistent overidentification with America's fantasmatic core, namely, the American Dream.

During the past decade, it has become somewhat fashionable to dismiss the American Dream as a myth that has lost its relevance as the unifying mythical narrative of the people of the United States. In his book *Dead Elvis*, Greil Marcus has already denounced the very concept as nothing more than a "now-horrible cliché" (1999, 129). The American Dream appears to have fallen into disrepute, and more recent book titles such as *Illusions of Opportunity* or *American Dream, American Nightmare* bear witness to the fact that its discontents seem to prevail over its promises. In one of the latest analyses to debunk the Dream, America does not even figure in the main title anymore: in Jeremy Rifkin's best-selling *The European Dream* (2004), he suggests that the American Dream, with its emphasis on the accumulation of personal wealth and the autonomy of the individual, is being eclipsed by a new set of values emerging on the other side of the Atlantic. But while Rifkin argues that a large percentage of Americans consider their national Dream to be an empty signifier, an immense amount of literature is still being published on its various incarnations. What is needed, though, is an analysis that would qualify as some sort of a theoretical account of the American Dream.

Another recent book to deal extensively with this undertheorized subject is Jim Cullen's *The American Dream: A Short History of an Idea That Shaped a Nation*. In his introduction, Cullen lists an impressive number of titles referring to the American Dream, but none of the books he looked at, he laments, "makes anything like a systematic attempt to define the term or trace its origin; its definition is virtually taken for granted" (2003, 5). Now, it is true that Cullen traces the etymological origins of the term, but then his prime concern is restricted to the specific contents that were projected onto this Dream at various periods in history. Reading it as a container of ideals, hopes, and promises, he disregards its structural properties as a form of public discourse that produces a specific kind of American subjectivity. One of the premises of my book is that ultimately the subject of the American Dream is constituted by the belief that the self can be endlessly remade for the sake of success and happiness.

There have been no efforts thus far to seriously theorize the American Dream in terms of its discursive structure. Even though everyone acknowledges that the idea has become increasingly vague, there still seems to be something self-evident about it that prevents the most basic questions from being raised. With *The European Dream*, Jeremy Rifkin inadvertently offers the perfect example for this kind of overfamiliarity with the term. Noting that the American Dream is originally a set of old European ideals that have long become calcified in the United States, he coins the concept of a new European Dream to refer to the sociopolitical currents that may transform the European Union into some sort of "United States of Europe." While I would not want to question Rifkin's general argument, the critical detail for me is the fact that his book is based on a false analogy. There is no such thing as a European Dream, and of course Rifkin is fully aware of this. But the crucial point is that the very notion of a *dream* has never been as deeply entrenched in its social and political structure in Europe as in America. In Europe, you dream at night, in the private corridors of your mind. In the United States, dreaming has always been very much a public affair and a fundamental constituent of America's national identity.

The vital question, then, is this: what does it mean that the American Dream is called a *dream?* More precisely, what are the implications if the American people are bound together by a mythical narrative that they refer to as a dream? This question articulates the blind spot of any historical account such as Cullen's, who focuses on the contents of the American Dream rather than on its structure. After all, ever since Sigmund Freud's *The Interpretation of Dreams* (originally published in 1900), we know that what is most significant about any dream is not its actual content, or the latent dream-thought that is concealed in the formations of this content; rather, the truly crucial aspect is the censoring instance that works like a filter between the two, modifying what Freud calls the latent dream-thought into the manifest formations of the dream. Hence, any structural analysis of the American Dream must take into account the Freudian insight that a dream is more than just a set of values, or ideals, that are molded into a mythical narrative. What is always at stake in a dream is that it is produced by an instance of censorship that transforms antagonisms of reality.

From here follows another crucial observation that may at first seem too banal to raise any notice. In the way it structures the social imaginary, the American Dream functions like a daydream. As Freud points out in "Creative Writers and Day-Dreaming" ([1908] 1959), every daydream is basically a fantasy, and as such it stages a scene of wish fulfillment that is usually kept secret from other people. Clearly, the communal fantasy that is the American daydream is not one of those intimate daydreams that one keeps to oneself; rather it functions as a public discourse, informing the social imaginary at large. Consciously shared by the people of the United States, the American Dream is a collective daydream. It is *the* collective daydream that constitutes America's identity as a nation.

To take this one step further, Freud notes that happy persons do not fantasize; only the unsatisfied are prone to daydreaming: "The motive forces of phantasies are unsatisfied wishes, and every single phantasy is the fulfilment of a wish, a correction of unsatisfying reality" (146). Thus, if the American Dream is a collective fantasy, not only does it produce a specifically American mode of subjectivity but it also represents an imaginary *correction* of social reality, and in this sense it is a public discourse that serves an ideological function. As a communal daydream, it offers an imaginary resolution of the antagonisms that pervade American society, and this is precisely what makes it an ideology.

Andy Kaufman enacted this daydream in such a consistent way as to give away the internal contradictions of this ideology. Hence, my reading of Kaufman is based on a sort of short-circuit between his performance work and that monumental cultural fantasy I identify as the American Dream. To paraphrase Slavoj Žižek, whose work provides the main theoretical framework for my study, I suggest that Kaufman offered a critique of the dream-ideology by staging it in a way that "estranged" America from the "self-evidence of its established identity" as the proverbial land of limitless opportunities (1992, 91). By totally identifying with the ideology of the American Dream, Kaufman articulated its internal contradictions.

I begin my analysis with a brief survey of the testimonials of sheer bafflement that accompanied Kaufman's entire career as an entertainer. In chapter 1 I recount the debate regarding his doubtful status within the genre of comedy, focusing on how this debate revealed a curious tendency to avoid accepting Kaufman as a specifically American phenomenon. Struggling to come to terms with his perplexing performances, Kaufman's contemporaries preferred to align him with various European avant-garde movements, thereby removing his work from the cultural topography where it actually took place. Though everyone seemed to agree that there was a radical edge to Kaufman's work, nobody was able to say what exactly this alleged radicality consisted in. Noting how *Man on the Moon* recovered the enigma that was Kaufman, I argue that Milos Forman's film "recoded" his work in a way that made it possible to grasp Kaufman's radical agenda beyond the avant-gardist notion of transgression.

Chapter 2 deals with the misleading lack of openly political material in Kaufman's work. Reading his performances against the backdrop of Lenny Bruce as one of the most eminently political artists in the history of stand-up comedy, I develop a theoretical framework to introduce Kaufman's radically different, and possibly more potent, logic of cultural criticism. As the central concept that informs my perspective on Kaufman, I invoke Slavoj Žižek's notion of the "overorthodox author" who absolutely complies with predominant ideological discourses and who may thus pose a much more radical threat to these ideologies than any transgressive artist would. Here I formulate my principal thesis that Andy Kaufman was precisely such an "overorthodox" performer. As the fundamentalist American Dreamer, he enacted America's communal fantasy in such a literal fashion as to render visible its fundamental inconsistencies.

In "Interlude: The American Dream," I offer a theoretical account of the American Dream and its discursive structure as an ideological apparatus. Based on the notion of ideology as theorized by Louis Althusser and Slavoj Žižek, I argue that there are two fundamental axes to every version of the American Dream, and these may be traced back to the foundational documents of the United States. First, the American Dream designates an imaginary objective that is accessible for every subject; this comprises what is generally referred to as the "myth of success," and by implication this entails a democratic promise of stardom—and in the final consequence, the prospect of symbolic immortality. The second axis functions on a more fundamental level of subjectivity, offering the possibility of a constant re-creation of one's self as a means to reach the imaginary objective of the first axis.

In chapters 3 and 4, I read Andy Kaufman's career along these lines of serial subjectivity and celebrity culture. Dealing with his most significant performances on stage and on television, I show how Kaufman mounted a seriously deconstructionist critique of the American dream-ideology by fulfilling its promises totally on his own, thus taking it more literally than it is prepared to be taken. Including comparative readings with Andy Warhol and Woody Allen's film *Zelig*, chapter 3 traces Kaufman's performances of himself as a "serial subject." This hysterical dissolution of his self, I argue, is what made his work so perplexing, or even unbearably traumatic, to the American public. In chapter 4 I discuss Kaufman's work in terms of the "democracy of stardom" as represented by the American Dream. While Kaufman offered preemptive parodies of America's obsession with celebrity in conceptual routines such as the "Has-Been Corner," his short-lived career as a wrestler confirms his literalist stance regarding the American democracy of stardom.

Finally, "Epitaph," the final section of the book, analyzes the intricacies of death and stardom as articulated in Kaufman's notorious acts of self-immolation. Reading his suicidal gestures as a necessary effect of his literal enactment of the American Dream, I argue that Kaufman rendered visible the uncanny flipside of the democracy of stardom as implied in the Dream. In concluding with a cross-reading with Elvis Presley, I point out why Kaufman, paradoxically, was more faithful in his enactment of the American Dream than Elvis, yet also less successful in fulfilling its promise of immortality. This is why, in the end, this book is not about comedy, but about death.

Ultimately, then, this book is about Andy Kaufman as an incarnation of the uncanny kernel of America's social imaginary. My reading of his performance work suggests that the real deadlock of the dream-ideology is *not* the fact "that any American Dream is finally too incomplete a vessel to contain longings that elude human expression or comprehension," as Jim Cullen so loftily phrases it in his history of the American Dream (2003, 182). In the final instance, the real problem is not just a question of limited capacity. As Kaufman's enactment of the American Dream makes clear, the discursive structure of this daydream is such that it actually evacuates the subject, leaving him in a state between the immortal and the dead.

Acknowledgments

Unlike the usual dream, the American Dream is less a private affair than a communal formation. To some extent, the same is true for this book, which would not have been possible without generous support from a number of friends and colleagues. I would like to thank Professor Elisabeth Bronfen at the University of Zurich, who has greatly inspired my thinking and who encouraged me to go along with this in the first place. I am most grateful to my dear friend Daniela Janser, whose theoretical support and criticism were essential to this project from very early on; without her, this book simply would not be what it is now. Some of the crucial arguments in this text were first developed in conversations with her and Veronika Grob. I am especially grateful to Scott Loren for his input upon reading the first draft of this book, and to Dr. Misha Kavka for reading portions of the final manuscript. Finally, I am much obliged to Professor Corina Caduff at the School of Art and Design Zurich for giving me the opportunity to complete the book, and I thank Andrea Kleinhuber at the University of Minnesota Press for making it happen. To all of them, in the words of Foreign Man: "Tenk you veddy much."

CHAPTER 1

Funny or Not

It's like what they say about stand-up: when it's funny
you're a comedian, when you're not it's performance art.

—Todd Solondz

In Milos Forman's underrated biopic *Man on the Moon* (1999),
comedian Andy Kaufman is depicted as an entertainer whose personal identity is endlessly dissimulated behind the multiplicity of
his personae. In what is arguably his most impressive performance
to date, Jim Carrey plays Andy Kaufman in a way that radically
dissipates any notion of positive and coherent subjectivity. This
permanent deferral of any consistent identity is the primary theoretical thrust of the film, and every figuration of Kaufman leaves
us to conclude that "this is not Andy Kaufman, but neither is this,
nor this," and so on. Kaufman as portrayed in *Man on the Moon*
is consistently multiple to the extent that one is unable to pinpoint the exact "location" of any real self among the numerous
"faces" displayed by his various personae. Thus, with a poignancy
unmatched in recent mainstream cinema, Forman's film effectively
stages one of the central theses (or clichés, for that matter) of
postmodernist theory, namely, the death of the subject.

Andy Kaufman's performance work has always been notoriously elusive. From his first club acts as a stand-up comedian in
the early 1970s, to his work on television, until his early death in
1984 (and even beyond), Kaufman inspired discussions about his

status within the context of comedy, and stand-up in particular. Hired to play Latka on the hugely successful television sitcom *Taxi* (1978–83), he became one of the most popular comic performers in America, but otherwise his performances were strangely out of the ordinary as far as comedy was concerned. When Kaufman *was* funny, people had difficulty explaining what it was exactly that made them laugh. When he was not, his presence was perplexing, uncanny, even infuriating.[1]

In *The Last Laugh*, Phil Berger's near-encyclopedic "portrait gallery" of stand-up comedy, one of the more honestly desperate attempts to come to terms with Kaufman is credited to *New York Times* critic Richard F. Shepard, who wrote about one of Kaufman's early comedy club acts that his work simply "defies categorization" (2000, 407). Likewise, Berger himself describes Kaufman as "a comic who resisted definition, a performer who seemed to take perverse pride in breaking down the accepted standards by which funnymen are judged" (402). The crucial trouble with Andy Kaufman, though, is that one cannot even be sure if the category of "funnyman" still applies, as he was constantly heading for performances that are beyond the distinction between what is considered funny and what is not. As Berger significantly phrases it, Kaufman's acts were often uncannily "beyond laughter."[2]

Peter Chelsom's film *Funny Bones* (1995) offers a very concise account of what it means to be funny by profession. Toward the end of the film, we witness the decisive dispute between Tommy (played by Oliver Platt), an aspiring, but hopelessly inept young stand-up comedian, and his father, an ageing comedy star. The father is played by real-life comedian Jerry Lewis, who, as in Martin Scorsese's film of the same title, functions as some sort of *King of Comedy* in this film. In *Funny Bones*, the Jerry Lewis character possesses the symbolic mandate to teach the ultimate paternal lesson to his son Tommy, who has proven a complete failure at his Las Vegas debut at the beginning of the film. The lesson in this dispute is that according to the supreme judgment of Tommy's father, there are only two types of comedians: "There's a funny bones comedian, and a non–funny bones comedian. They're both funny. One *is* funny. The other *tells* funny."

This categorical distinction uttered "in the name of the father" is clearly addressed as a death sentence for the son, as the paternal "King of Comedy" goes on to say that Tommy, unfortunately, is neither. Not only is he not intrinsically funny, but he has not even learned how to "tell funny." By declaring Tommy fundamentally unfunny, the Jerry Lewis character asserts, and effectively executes, the symbolic death of his son within his own domain, which is the realm of comedy. Of course, the Oedipal revenge is inevitable: Later on, Tommy denounces his father's entire career as a product of plagiarism—the huge success of the supposedly infallible paternal figure turns out to be based on material that the Jerry Lewis character had illegitimately adopted from his English family of variety artistes before he left for the New World to reinvent himself as America's King of Comedy.

This brief account of what is played out in *Funny Bones* reflects some of the central issues of the work of Andy Kaufman, and it serves as some sort of blueprint for me to outline what is at stake in my analysis of Kaufman's performances. Clearly, the first and most basic convergence lies in the fact that with Kaufman, too, the question of his funniness as a performer had always been a subject of public debate. Unlike the junior comedian in *Funny Bones*, though, Kaufman's failures to live up to the standards of comedy were usually regarded as self-induced.

As Philip Auslander points out in *Presence and Resistance*, his study on postmodernist American performance, the traditional interpretation as reiterated in the popular press was not that Kaufman was in any way "redefining stand-up comedy." Rather, the standard perspective was "that he was intentionally courting failure as a comic by refusing to be 'funny,' an interpretation tacitly endorsed by Kaufman himself, who frequently claimed never to have told a joke in his professional life" (1992, 141–42). In fact, Kaufman always went to great lengths to dissociate his performances from the standards of comedy, claiming that none of his acts was ever meant to be funny: "I've never really done what they call 'straight comedy,'" he points out in *The Midnight Special* (1981). And in a heartbreaking scene from a show at the Catskills in New York (extracts of which are published on a DVD entitled *The Real Andy Kaufman*), the self-assigned noncomedian seems on the verge of tears, as he is desperately begging for the sympathy of his audience: "I've never claimed to be a comedian. I've never claimed to be able to tell a joke. I've never been able to tell a joke."[3]

This stance is curiously at odds with the basic imperative of "straight" stand-up as defined by Kaufman in *The Midnight Special:* "Comedians would go up and do twenty minutes of joke-telling." Clearly, the joke is the defining unit of stand-up comedy.[4] As John Limon states in his book *Stand-Up Comedy in Theory, or, Abjection in America*, "stand-up is dominated by mini-climaxes—the series of punch lines" (2000, 9). With Kaufman, there was no such series of comic climaxes, and despite the fact that he originally emerged from the performance context of stand-up comedy, he often declared that laughter was not what he was after. According to Bill Zehme's exquisite biography *Lost in the Funhouse*, Kaufman explicitly pointed out that none of his acts offered any kind of punchline (2001, 172). In short, here was a funny man who refused to act funny. But was it really that simple?

After all, the absence of a punchline does not necessarily imply that an act is not funny, as is illustrated by a "joke" from Kaufman's Foreign Man character, undoubtedly the most popular of his various stage personae.[5] As part of *The Andy Kaufman*

Special (1977), Foreign Man tells a story about two boys and a girl who work very hard to carry a large cannon onto the highest mountain in Spain; when they finally reach the top, though, they realize that they forgot to take the cannonball with them, because each of them thought that one of the others had it. With his exotic accent, Foreign Man presents this vignette as if it actually did fulfill the formal requirements of a joke. Manically gesturing with excitement, he asks the public to hold their laughter and wait for the punchline, while in fact, there is no punchline to come. Just like the two boys and the girl who climb a mountain with a cannon but do not have the cannonball with them to load it, Foreign Man works hard to deliver a joke without having a punchline.

Foreign Man fails miserably as a joker, since he tells an anecdote that is structurally unfunny—still, the laughter from the audience suggests that Foreign Man, for his part, is not unfunny at all. As Limon argues in his analysis of Lenny Bruce, such non-jokes told in a comedy context are always meta-jokes in the sense that they reflect back upon their own formal terms, and upon jokes themselves. In a somewhat feeble twist of argument, Limon tautologically notes that in the case of these nonfunny meta-jokes, "what the audience is finding funny is that it finds this funny" (2000, 18). As regards Foreign Man, a more persuasive explanation as to why he is funny is provided by Freud's seminal text *Jokes and Their Relation to the Unconscious*. In his discussion of the mode of comicality, Freud summarizes his argument as follows:

> Thus a uniform explanation is provided of the fact that a person appears comic to us if, in comparison with ourselves, he makes too great an expenditure on his bodily functions and too little on his mental ones; and it cannot be denied that in both cases our laughter expresses a pleasurable sense of the superiority which we feel in relation to him. (1905, 195)

Kaufman's Foreign Man character is funny because he is "guilty" on both charges: he physically works too hard to produce less than a joke. It is true that in terms of the categorical distinction from *Funny Bones*, Foreign Man is not even able to "tell funny"—but it is precisely his inability to "tell funny" that makes him funny nonetheless, as he overcompensates for his "mental" insufficiency by means of excessive body movements.

Considering the crudely phallic symbolism of the cannon and the missing cannonball, Foreign Man's nonjoke may also be read as a failed example of what Freud calls an "*obscene* joke," which serves "the purpose of exposure" (1905, 97, italics in original). For example, if poor Foreign Man were to state that the boys wanted to "shoot their cannon, but they didn't have the balls," then at least his story would contain some aspect of exposure in Freud's sense, but since Foreign Man persistently uses the word "*cannon*ball," what could have been a (weak) joke of obscenity is now merely an impotent one.

Hence, Kaufman's Foreign Man character embraces his own impotence as far as the codes of stand-up comedy are concerned. In this sense, Andy Kaufman also deals with exclusion from the domain of comedy, but in contrast to the scene of filial castration from *Funny Bones*, there is no paternal figure present that would sanction, or execute, Foreign Man's symbolic exclusion from the domain of comedy. Instead of the father, the comedian himself is in charge here, and ultimately, this brief scenario turns into a gleeful celebration of an act of self-castration.

Paradoxically, Foreign Man was the closest Andy Kaufman ever got to what he would call "straight" comedy. As for Kaufman himself, he often flatly refused to be listed under the category of any sort of comedy: "I never claim to be a funny man, a comedian, or even a talented man" (Zehme 2001, 140–41). Instead Kaufman found himself an altogether different designation for his type of entertainment when he started to refer to himself as a "song-and-dance man," which would become one of his most famous stock phrases. As with authors of literary texts, though, one of the problems with this kind of self-definition is that any performer's statement about his representational agenda is to be treated with caution. On top of that, the particular trouble with Andy Kaufman is that it has always been notoriously difficult to tell the artist's self from his various stage personae. Hence, if someone whom we presume to be Andy Kaufman declares himself to be a "song-and-dance man" rather than a comedian, this can hardly be taken at face value, because you never know "who" is talking. Kaufman tends to disappear behind the array of his masks and characters, and this is what became the topical focus of *Man on the Moon*.

Here is a Hollywood film that denies any presence of the protagonist in the sense of a singular subject that would answer if one were to call on him. In some sense, this postmodernist thesis of *Man on the Moon* represents a more sophisticated version of another standard interpretation of Kaufman, whose dissolution of selves was regularly explained away by reference to schizo-phrenia or multiple personality disorder. As Bill Zehme notes, the

"Hello. I am Andy." Jim Carrey as Andy Kaufman as Foreign Man in the opening sequence of *Man on the Moon* (Universal Pictures, 1999).

popular press often focused on Kaufman's "crises of identity."[6] Accordingly, Tony Danza, one of Kaufman's fellow actors in the television sitcom *Taxi*, reports in the documentary *I'm from Hollywood* (1989) that Kaufman "was supposed to have split personalities." This focus on a supposed psychological disorder informed the perspectives on Kaufman to the degree that his most significant performance work "raised more questions about his sanity than his artistry," as Michael Nash succinctly puts it in his essay "Andy Kaufman's Last Laugh" (1990, 2). When performance practices are explained in terms of clinical pathology, this is usually an unmistakable sign that something uncanny is at stake.

The Patchwork Avant-Gardist

Clearly, there have always been more refined strategies to come to terms with Kaufman's truly perplexing presence, but even the most cursory catalogue of the labels and cross-references used by his contemporaries cannot fail to show a sense of utter helplessness. As the popular press as well as his colleagues sensed that Kaufman's performance work was curiously "other than comedy," they often resorted to finding equivalent artists beyond the comedy context. Thus, Bill Zehme cites *Saturday Night Live* producer Lorne Michaels, for whom Kaufman's act of lip-synching the theme song from the *Mighty Mouse* cartoon series (though only in parts) on the very first segment of his comedy show captured nothing less than "the essence of avant-garde" (2001, 161). Along similar lines, comedian Carl Reiner, upon watching one of Kaufman's comedy club performances for the first time, "quickly realized" that he was witness to "something very unusual and historic in comedy theater" (166). Still, one is left to wonder as to what it was exactly that made Kaufman "historic" and "unusual," or the "essence of avant-garde."

In terms of cultural theory, Lorne Michaels's reference to some sort of avant-gardist thrust in Kaufman's work may be rather casual, but it is still crucial here, as it appears in various forms in the popular press as well as in statements from Kaufman's fellow comedians. Zehme, for instance, cites comedian Richard Belzer, who considers Andy Kaufman a "performance artist before the term existed," while in the eyes of Richard Lewis, Kaufman "was almost like Ionesco doing stand-up" (139). Among journalists, this quest for avant-gardist equivalents for Kaufman seemed to expand into some sort of competition for the most concise, or extravagant, intertextual reference. In an article for *Time* magazine, an author named Tony Clifton entered this game of cross-references, describing Andy Kaufman as "comedy's stand-up Pirandello" (1979, 78).[7] Two years later, the same journal featured an article from Richard Corliss, who offered a more elaborate comparison to avant-garde art when he referred to Kaufman as the "Duchampian *agent provocateur* of modern comedy: the Dada of ha-ha" (1981, 87, italics in original). There seemed to be no limits to this cross-referential competition with avant-garde terminology.

The curious thing about these cross-references is that in some way or another, they all fit, and none of them seems totally out of place or downright inappropriate. But then again, nearly all of these keywords function as empty signifiers that simply refer to what one is unable to come to terms with. So why not extend the chain of analogies even further? For example, consider the end of Kaufman's show at Carnegie Hall, when he announced that ten buses were waiting outside to take everybody from the audience for a midnight snack of milk and cookies. Does this not evoke the art Happenings around 1960, which dissolved the conventionally frontal relation between a work of art and the viewer, creating situational "environments" that did not even involve acts of performance art, let alone the presence of an "art object"?[8]

Or take the very beginning of *The Midnight Special*, when Kaufman addresses his audience in the lyrical gibberish of the nonexistent language of Caspiar, Foreign Man's imaginary home country. Does this not suggest that Kaufman was some sort of *lettriste*, and thus may easily be aligned with yet another avant-gardist movement, namely, the Internationale Situationniste as initiated by Guy Debord and his comrades-in-arms? As Roberto Ohrt points out in *Phantom Avantgarde*, the primary target of Debord's project was to produce "irritations of reality" (1990, 177, my translation), and, in this sense, Kaufman surely qualifies as a true situationist, as he frequently disturbed the public's sense of what is real and what is not.

One could carry on like this forever, but the result of these cross-references is that Kaufman is effectively turned into some sort of *patchwork avant-gardist*. It may be true that such comparisons with avant-garde artists like Ionesco, Pirandello, the Dadaists (or Debord, for that matter) may be helpful to convey a preliminary impression to anyone who is not familiar with Kaufman's work. Also, it might be a valid premise to state that Kaufman was to stand-up comedy what Pirandello was to the domain of traditional theater, or that he appropriated Ionesco's absurdist theater in an effort to rework it in terms of the pop-cultural context of American comedy. Indeed, these supposed analogies might very well work as theoretical perspectives for an analysis of Kaufman's performance work—but beyond their superficial "truth claims," what all these cross-references clearly betray is a curious tendency to evade this performer as a specifically American cultural phenomenon.

Every comparison to any of these (predominantly European) avant-garde movements involves a conspicuous and even slightly suspicious gesture of turning away from America as that specific cultural topography from which Andy Kaufman actually emerged and where his performances took place. In the entertainment industry, stressing any performer's alleged affinity with avant-gardist high-brow culture is arguably the easiest strategy to stigmatize artists whose work is experienced as troublesome for some reason or another. Thus, while it has always been perfectly clear that Kaufman was some kind of an "extremist" in the context of America, as his producer George Shapiro has pointed out (Zehme 2001, 257), there is still a curious lack of analytic work that tries to theorize this supposed "extremism" specifically in terms of American culture. And while it has been all but common sense that there was a certain subversive edge in many of Kaufman's performances, there are still hardly any theoretical accounts on the question as to what this alleged edge of subversion truly consisted in.[9]

In part, this conspicuous lack of analytic work on a performer who is now widely recognized as one of the seminal American artists of postmodern times may be due to Kaufman's notorious volatility in terms of cultural genre. As for his status in comparison with the fellow comedians of his generation, Bill Zehme argues that Kaufman "was theater whereas they told jokes—but he belonged with them; there was nowhere else to put him. It was the only context in which he made sense, not that he made sense, not that he ever tried" (2001, 138). However, this latter claim regarding the deliberately nonsensical nature of Kaufman's performances is ultimately no different from any of the previously mentioned comments from his contemporaries. After all, the reference to sheer nonsense is just another indication of a failure to come to terms with Kaufman. Whether his work is considered nonsense, comic avant-garde, or simply the product of a pathological schizo, it all adds up to the fact that America was unable to make sense of Kaufman.

This kind of failed signification is one of the crucial points in Hal Foster's book *The Return of the Real* (1996), where he argues that the advent of any avant-garde is typically marked by the *failure to signify*. In his effort to theorize and revalidate the notion of avant-garde for the end of the twentieth century, Foster takes recourse to Freudian trauma theory, arguing that the work of avant-garde "is never historically effective or fully significant in its initial moments. It cannot be because it is traumatic—a hole in the symbolic order of its time that is not prepared for it" (29). One of the purposes of this book is to point out in what way this is also true for Andy Kaufman, the noncomedian who supposedly represented the "essence of avant-garde," to use the casual remark from Lorne Michaels. In my reading of Kaufman, the notion of avant-garde is maintained as an implicit theoretical tool, but in order to focus on America as the cultural site of Kaufman's performance work, I shall largely refrain from relating him back to any historical avant-garde movement or event. In short, the concept of avant-garde is to be thought of as no more or less than the particular structure of the failed signification described by Hal Foster.

If this is not a book on laughter or comedy, then the reason is not that comedians "tell jokes," whereas Andy Kaufman was "theater," as Bill Zehme would have it. While one should not understand Kaufman's claim to be a song-and-dance man too literally, his denial that he is a comedian should still be taken seriously. At the outset of this analysis, I will briefly situate Kaufman within the context of comedy, but the focus will not be on genre, nor on humor—thus following Michael Nash, who has pointed out that Kaufman's work is arguably "best understood as performance art" (1990, 5).[10] One of the very few articles on Kaufman to be published in an art context, Nash's essay "Andy Kaufman's Last Laugh" prepared the grounds for a perspective on Kaufman that transcends the contextual confines of comedy, just as Andy Kaufman did in his artistic practice both on stage and on television.

In his short essay, Nash discusses Kaufman within the framework of television theory, but more important, he aligns him with the strategies of postmodernist conceptual art. Arguing that Kaufman transformed conceptual art into popular culture by way of stand-up comedy and television, Nash claims that just as "conceptual art is about art, Kaufman's conceptual comedy was ultimately about comedy" (5). While one may disagree on his apodictic claim that Kaufman's performances were, in effect, a form of meta-comedy, Nash acknowledges that Kaufman went beyond a critical interrogation of merely the formal conventions of stand-up comedy, offering a more fundamental critique of the codes of entertainment, and television.

Drawing on Nash's pioneering article, Philip Auslander pursues a similar line of argument in the chapters that are dedicated to Kaufman in his aforementioned study *Presence and Resistance*, which provides the most elaborate interpretation of Kaufman's work to date. Following Nash, Auslander chooses to discuss Kaufman not in terms of stand-up comedy proper, but within the theoretical context of postmodernist performance art, arguing that there is a striking affinity linking Kaufman's disarticulation of the self to the position of performance theorists such as Chantal Pontbriand and Josette Féral. For instance, Auslander cites Féral, for whom postmodernist performance art deals with an "absence of meaning" as produced by a "machine working with serial signifiers" (1992, 46). Indeed, does this not read like a concise formula for what is at stake with the supposedly nonsensical entertainment machine called Andy Kaufman, who kept reproducing serial versions of himself, discarding any notion of a coherent self?

In the main strand of his argument, though, Auslander expands on the analogy suggested by Nash, reading Kaufman's work with conceptual art of the 1960s and early 1970s. For instance, he argues that Kaufman's "intentional infantilism," which he exhibited in many of his performances, bears a profound affinity to the work from conceptual artists such as Vito Acconci or Alison

Knowles in the sense that it seems like a rejection of his virtuosity as a performer (1992, 141). As for one of Kaufman's notorious sing-along acts, namely, his integral (!) rendition of "One Hundred Bottles of Beer on the Wall," Auslander states that in a fashion similar to Acconci's works of conceptual performance art, Kaufman's conceptual comedy acts "were often structured as repetitive tests of endurance—his own and the audience's" (140).

As another example for these conceptualist "tests of endurance," let me briefly evoke a second incident that serves as an even more radical illustration of what Nash calls Kaufman's critique of the relationships between performer, audience, and context. In his biography, Bill Zehme reports a two-hour show at a college in Tampa, at the end of which Kaufman uttered one of the most ritualized addresses from an entertainer to his audience: "I want to thank each and every one of you." On this particular occasion, though, Andy Kaufman reportedly took this conventional expression of a performer's gratitude to his audience by its word. Literally enacting what is supposed to be nothing but an empty symbolic gesture, Kaufman "walked down off of the stage and shook hands with each and every one of them. It took the better part of another hour to do this. He said 'Thank you' every time" (2001, 234). This scene not only questions the conventional relationship between the entertainer and his audience, but it shows Kaufman as a performer who faithfully enacts what is commonly understood as an empty rhetorical gesture. Thus, it prefigures the notion of literalism, which will be one of the crucial points of my thesis about Kaufman.

But for now, let me briefly return to Auslander's analysis, the specific focus of which is on Kaufman's performance art as a deconstructionist critique of a tradition of performance that privileges presence. According to Auslander, "Kaufman's conceptual project was to put his own presence and authority as a performer radically at risk" (1992, 140). What his performance work ulti-mately amounts to, then, would be a genuinely postmodernist refusal of presence as a result of the way Kaufman persistently blurred any "distinction between his performance personae and himself" (55). In short, Auslander argues that Kaufman was a de-constructionist artist who radically put into question his own status as a performer.

From this perspective, the snappy tabloid term of the "Kamikaze Comic" (Nash 1990, 3) suddenly seems uncomfortably appropriate in the very literal sense of its implication of suicide. In terms of the risks he took in his performances, Kaufman truly was "a man bent on destroying himself in public," as Zehme argues in his biography (2001, 289)—and this is the point where I return to the scene from *Funny Bones* mentioned above, where the young comedian is declared unfunny, hence symbolically castrated, by word of his father, the comedy star. As for Andy Kaufman, one could interpret his entire career as a series of such symbolic deaths within the domain of comedy, or even within the wider cultural frame of American show business at large. Still, there is one crucial difference to the scene from *Funny Bones*, in that Kaufman's deaths were not declared by word of a paternal figure, but they were always self-executed, or at least self-induced, provoked by himself. Thus, Kaufman's most significant acts were radically suicidal in terms of his authority as a performer—and as *Man on the Moon* has made explicit, Kaufman's performances were also suicidal in terms of his subjectivity.

Andy Kaufman Recoded

If every avant-garde constitutes a traumatic failure to signify, *Man on the Moon* designates the moment when Andy Kaufman was reintegrated into popular culture. As this Hollywood film re-kindled interest for Kaufman on a massive scale, the "patchwork avant-gardist" was finally recuperated as a mass-cultural phenomenon. Thus, Milos Forman's biopic represents precisely that "second event" which, according to Foster, "recodes" and restructures the primary trauma of avant-garde (1996, 29). In this case, the original-historical Andy Kaufman represents the primary event of failed signification, and *Man on the Moon* provides the momentum of deferred action (what Freud terms *Nachträglichkeit*) that enables us to "make sense" of Kaufman's performance work in a way that may not have registered at the time of its production.[11]

As noted above, *Man on the Moon* portrays Kaufman in a way that effectively turns him into an uncanny embodiment of the dead subject of postmodernism. This central thesis of Forman's film serves as my starting point to reflect back on what we may now appropriately term Kaufman's performance art. Hence, this perspective is informed, and therefore necessarily inflected, by the belated refiguration of Kaufman as depicted in *Man on the Moon*. My project is based on a process of retroactive formation, as it was triggered by a cinematic after-image of the actual object of my analysis, which is Kaufman, not Forman's biopic. As this reading of Kaufman's work is always "under the spell" of *Man on the Moon*, it entails a potentially precarious conflation of biography, performance, and the cinematic fiction that was derived from Kaufman's career.

In her book *Quoting Caravaggio*, Mieke Bal has put forth a compelling theoretical framework to deal with this kind of retroactive exchange. Stating the premise for her concept of "preposterous history," she draws attention to the way "the work performed by later images obliterates the older images as they were before that intervention and creates new versions of old images instead" (1999, 1). In this perspective of what Bal terms "preposterous history," that which is historically older emerges as an aftereffect of the way in which it was subsequently reworked, and this certainly applies for the way *Man on the Moon* relates to the historical phenomenon that was Andy Kaufman. However "factual" or "authentic" Forman's cinematic resurrection of Andy Kaufman may claim to be, this creation of a fictional after-image must also be thought of as a historical intervention that obliterates the images of the real Kaufman *as they were before.*

In this respect, the original Andy Kaufman is always also (and can never be other than) an aftereffect of the later version of Andy Kaufman as embodied by Jim Carrey in *Man on the Moon.* But in the sense that my reading focuses on a historical entertainment artist who has been permanently dis-figured by the new images from Forman's biopic, it entails a productive exercise in what Bal terms "preposterous history." Arguably, it is precisely this interplay between Kaufman and his cinematic after-image that promises to illuminate the blind spots of earlier perspectives, producing insights that lead beyond the bafflement of Kaufman's contemporaries.

This study owes yet another debt to Mieke Bal in that it is very much informed by her perspective on contemporary art as a form of cultural philosophy. In a fashion similar to the way *Quoting Caravaggio* is ultimately "about how art thinks" (22), this book deals with Kaufman's performances as "theoretical objects," treating them as "instances of cultural philosophy" (5) that "think," or "theorize," American culture in the context of popular entertainment. Thus, my thesis on Kaufman's body of work evolves from the basic idea that his dissipation of any coherent identity must not be read as an index of some private libidinal obsessions on the part of this particular entertainer, let alone as a product of an "identity crisis" or any other psychological disorder that Kaufman was often said to suffer from. Instead, the dissimulation of his self in an array of personae is read as an effect of how his performances relate to America's social imaginary.

In this context, a phrase from *Los Angeles Times* critic Howard Rosenberg unwittingly offers a hint as to what might truly be at stake in Kaufman's acts. Rosenberg describes Kaufman's comedy in the sense that it "consists of reality and fantasy rolled up into one big put-on" (Zehme 2001, 294). Theoretically sloppy and vague as this remark may be, it provides one of the keywords for my study, namely, fantasy. In some sense, one of the prime concerns of this book is to translate into more psychoanalytical terms a notion offered by Phil Berger, who describes Andy Kaufman quite simply as a "fantasist" (2000, 405). The fantasy enacted by Andy Kaufman, I argue, is the communal daydream that is commonly referred to as the American Dream.

Andy Kaufman's entire career on stage as well as on television may be read along the lines of an enactment of those mythical narratives implied in the American Dream. Whether willfully or by some sort of "naive" misconception, Kaufman staged an understanding of the American Dream as a "real" biographical narrative that may be enacted literally, fulfilling its promises by himself. And this is where we find another analogy to *Funny Bones*, where the Jerry Lewis character is evidently a product of the American Dream. As it turns out, he is originally from England, and his entire star status as King of Comedy is the result of an act of self-invention in the United States.

As is the case with any fantasy, however, the American Dream can only work in its ideological function as long as one keeps a certain distance to it. Andy Kaufman made this distance collapse—and ultimately, this is the unacknowledged center that is only cautiously touched upon by vague references such as Kaufman's alleged "extremism," or, again, the "essence of avant-garde." Kaufman's performances are not to be reduced to mere formal transgressions, avant-gardist innovations within the conventionalized limits of the theatrical form of comedy, as Philip Auslander would read them. Kaufman's mode of subversion was much more radical. If he was one of the most controversial figures in American show business, it was not because Kaufman was not "funny" or supposedly ceased to be funny at some point. Rather, it was his no-less-than-obscene gesture of absolute compliance with the imperative of that colossal collective fantasy that is the American Dream.

In his peculiar relation to the American Dream, Andy Kaufman may in fact turn out to be the true representative of what Greil Marcus, in his book *Dead Elvis*, argued about Elvis Presley. After all, he could as well be referring to Kaufman when he writes about Elvis as this "emptied, triumphantly vague symbol of displaced identity" (1991, 33). According to Marcus, the cultural phenomenon that was Elvis Presley not just bespeaks "the necessity existing in every culture that leads it to produce a perfect, all-inclusive metaphor for itself" (3). Elvis, he argues, is also

> a presentation, an acting out, a fantasy, a performance, not of what it means to be American—to be a creature of history, the inheritor of certain crimes, wars, ideas, landscapes—but rather a presentation, an acting out, a fantasy of what the deepest and most extreme possibilities and dangers of our national identity are. (31)

If this is what Elvis as a specifically American cultural phenomenon is all about, then this very same "presentation" is also at stake in Andy Kaufman's performance work. At the very beginning of his book, Marcus remarks that Elvis had swallowed more of America's internal contradictions than any other figure he can think of; in the final instance of my analysis, Kaufman will emerge as precisely that other figure, the most faithful embodiment of the paradoxes of the American dream-ideology. As a result of his persistent identification with the innermost fantasies of American culture, he confronted the public with the fact that the realization of their shared fantasy would imply the dissipation of the self and, consequently, may lead to the death of any sense of coherent subjectivity.

But another death will be involved, namely, the symbolic death of the comedian (or performance artist, for that matter) who physically enacts this fantasmatic narrative, taking the American Dream by its word. After all, death and comedy have always been intricately bound. In his essay on "Hitchcockian Suspense," Pascal Bonitzer argues that comedy (especially slapstick comedy and the animated cartoon) takes place in a "world of pure gesture," which is to say that "protagonists are in principle immortal and indestructible." According to Bonitzer, this entails that in these forms of comedy, violence is almost invariably "universal and inconsequential" (1992, 18). What this also implies, though, is that whenever a symbolic gesture is taken for real, the effects prove catastrophic.

In *Funny Bones*, a truly devastating flashback scene illustrates the tragic consequences of an empty gesture when it is executed literally—in the flesh, so to speak. One of the core scenes of the narrative features the young comedian's English half-brother Jack (played by Lee Evans) performing in his family's variety show. As part of his comedy act, he hits his villainous stage companion on the head with a newspaper rolled into some sort of stick—clearly, this is an instance of pure gestural slapstick violence that has no real consequences.

Yet the film then shows us that at some point, this comic feat went tragically wrong because the newspaper roll unexpectedly contained a little steel tube. As Jack smashed the head of his stage companion for real, what was supposed to be purely gestural turned into physical violence. This scene of brutal frenzy shows that slapstick comedy (and arguably, comedy at large) draws on a precarious reliance on the pure gesture of inconsequential violence. Whenever the gesture is enacted literally, it may impinge the flesh, and this is when comedy turns out to be lethal. With Andy Kaufman, though, the consequences are even more disturbing. In the final instance, his literal enactment of the American Dream points to something more horrifying than death.

CHAPTER 2

The Limits of Transgression

There are a finite number of jokes in the universe.

—Talking Heads, *Stop Making Sense*

In 1974 singer Barry Manilow gave a series of concerts in Philadelphia, and Andy Kaufman, as yet hardly known, was booked as his opening act. Manilow curiously recalls that Kaufman's performances had such an effect on the audience that during the entire week, Manilow's job as the headliner "was to try to bring them back from the edge of revolution" (Zehme 2001, 154). Of course, a recollection like this shows all the bearings of retroactive mythification, but however romanticized Manilow's account may be, there is a crucial point here about the politics of Andy Kaufman. As a performer, Kaufman never brought up any explicitly political concerns, either on stage or in any of his television appearances. If his performances produced outrage among his audience, as many of them did, and if he drove Manilow's concert audience to the "edge of revolution," none of the upsurge was ever due to any political stance in the strict sense of the word.

In fact, one of the most irritating aspects about Andy Kaufman may have been his near-obsessive preoccupation with harmless, infantile gestures. He would invite his audience to sing along with his version of "The Cow Goes Moo," and he frequently ended his shows performing Fabian Forte's "This Friendly World," a pacifying feel-good song if there ever was one and, in Bill Zehme's words, "a gentle anthem of kindness" (2001, 42). After his show at Carnegie Hall, Kaufman invited his audience out for a midnight snack of milk and cookies in the cafeteria at the New York School of Printing. Even when he was doing his breathtaking impression of Elvis Presley, he would wear a sweatshirt under his Elvis outfit that read "I LOVE GRANDMA," as if he wanted to make sure that the outrageous pelvic thrust of the King of Rock 'n' Roll was immediately put to rest.[1]

The only performance that ever saw Kaufman using openly political material occurred right at the outset of his Carnegie Hall show on April 26, 1979. As his own opening act, Kaufman entered the stage in the guise of Tony Clifton, his Vegas lounge-singer character, and intoned the national anthem in a mock-version that was terribly out of key. Zehme reports that while Tony Clifton was singing "The Star-Spangled Banner," a montage of pictures was "projected on a large movie screen behind him, including rippling flags, jet flyovers, missile detonations, goose-stepping Nazis, and Hitler himself" (2001, 253).[2] Clearly, this precarious metaphoric short-circuit connecting the symbolic domains of Nazi Germany and the United States of America is mildly offensive to say the least. Still, this crude montage of fascist imagery and the official anthem of the "land of the free" remains an erratic gesture in Kaufman's performance history, as it is the only instance in his entire career where he ventured for a stage act that explicitly "talked politics."[3]

But maybe a different perspective is required to study the rhetoric of Andy Kaufman. If his performances have always been devoid of any material that one could call political, then the purpose of this chapter is to prepare the theoretical basis for a perspective that looks beyond this blatantly apolitical rhetoric.

Sharpening the focus for the radical logic behind it Kaufman's lack of political material, I will attempt to re-envision him as a performer who engaged in a form of cultural critique that was truly radical in such a way as to stir American culture at its innermost.

The idea, then, is to seek a logic of subversion that would explain how the cultural phenomenon that was Andy Kaufman came to constitute a traumatic "failure to signify" in the mass-cultural context of American show business. Including a critical reading of Philip Auslander's study of Kaufman (arguably the most significant cultural analysis of Kaufman's performance work up to now), this chapter will lead into an interlude that will designate what may be called the cultural foil of this work—namely, the American Dream as the ideological text that was put to the test by Kaufman's performances.

From Transgression to Resistance (and Back Again)

In order to approach the radical kernel of Kaufman's seemingly uncritical comedy indirectly, it should prove helpful to start with a comedian who built himself a reputation for being eminently political, namely, Lenny Bruce. One of the first figures to violate the codes of conduct within the genre of stand-up, Lenny Bruce often took an openly political stance in his performances, and in the course of his stage career, he became more and more notorious for his behavior on stage. Thus, while he has long been widely appreciated as one of the harbingers of postmodern stand-up comedy, Bruce is also glorified as the "outrageous comedian par excellence" (Limon 2000, 13). In a similar vein, when Bruce is turned into a literary character in Don DeLillo's grand novel *Underworld*, he is introduced simply as "the infamous sick comic" (1997, 504). This is how Lenny Bruce is registered in America's cultural memory: outrageous, infamous, sick.

But what exactly was so scandalous about Lenny Bruce? In his aforementioned book on stand-up comedy, John Limon investigates the outrage of Lenny Bruce. Using Freudian psychoanalysis as his theoretical framework, Limon reads Bruce's transgressive comedy in terms of filiation and Oedipal struggles with the paternal order, but his analysis is also informed by Julia Kristeva's concept of the abject as theorized in her book *Powers of Horror* (1982). In the introductory chapter, Limon states his premise that "what is stood up in stand-up comedy is abjection" (2000, 4), and in Lenny Bruce, he spots the perfect figure to support this thesis. While many of Bruce's performances may have had an aggressive or even phallic thrust, his comedy of abjection ultimately amounted to an infantile threat against the codes of the paternal law. According to Limon, Bruce's comedy provoked outrage because he enacted an "excremental regression to infancy" (5), confronting the audience with an erection of infantile, presymbolic filth designed not only to threaten, but to degrade the paternal order.[4]

In the comedy of Lenny Bruce, Limon argues in the introduction of his book, the "abject gets erected and mobilized in the place of the phallus" (4). Accordingly, Limon's article on Lenny Bruce ends with his overly neat conclusion that in its last consequence, stand-up comedy is the "resurrection of your father as your child" (27). Therefore, the stand-up comic according to Limon does not exactly "kill" the keeper of the paternal mandate, because stand-up works on the assumption that the law is always already dead—but when the law is "resurrected" like a zombie, the comedian may punish and defile it with the abject filth on whose exclusion the paternal order was founded in the first place.

Thus, Lenny Bruce not only transgressed the classical codes of stand-up, but he aggressively teased the law. After all, the quintessential commonplace about this comedian of abjection is that both his topical "sickness" as well as his infamously frank use of "dirty" vocabulary repeatedly brought him in conflict with representatives of the law. As Limon points out, "Bruce turned every judge into a father, and every legal performance into an opportunity to seduce and poison the paternal ear" (26).[5] At closer inspection, though, Bruce's conflicts with the law turn out to have been more paradoxical than they seem at first. As regards Bruce's outrageousness as a stage performer, Limon points out that, interestingly enough, the only expressions of outrage apart from journalists were on the part of the legal system (18–19). As far as the enforcement of the law is concerned, the most significant aspect about Lenny Bruce is the conspicuous discrepancy between the agency of the law and the "people" in whose name it was supposed to intervene. Still based on Goldman's account, John Limon notes that "no member of an American audience ever brought a complaint against Bruce," and he concludes that the law acted totally on its own behalf (19, 23). So in the case of Lenny Bruce, the judicial apparatus curiously functioned as a representative of none other than itself, mechanically responding to Bruce's rhetorical offenses.

Thus, it seems that even though Lenny Bruce did violate the codes of the genre, his transgressions may have been purely formal gestures that failed to redefine the symbolic field or make the law collapse. On the contrary, insofar as his violations induced the law to operate on its own terms, one can say he actually courted its symbolic sanction. As Limon concludes in his essay on Bruce, the stand-up comedy of Lenny Bruce starts from an aggressive stance toward the audience, and this aggression is then submitted to the law: "The progress is to convert Audience to Law for the purpose of winning the Law back as Audience" (26). In the final instance, then, the "sick" comedy of Lenny Bruce actually "makes the law work."

Accordingly, Limon argues that Bruce's "biography as a comedian reads like a vain attempt not to overthrow the law but, by threatening it, to bring it into play" (25). In terms of how he relates to the law, Bruce curiously recalls the surrealists of the faction surrounding André Breton. As Hal Foster notes in *The Return of the Real*, Breton's group of surrealists frequently acted "like juvenile victims who provoked the paternal law *as if to ensure that it was still there*—at best in a neurotic plea for punishment, at worst in a paranoid demand for order" (1996, 159, italics in original). In this regard, Bruce's comedy shows an unexpected alliance with surrealism.

In contrast, the performance work of Andy Kaufman is often called surrealist, yet it is far from transgressive. This fundamental difference to Bruce's "dirty" comedy is nicely illustrated by Kaufman's response when the executive board at ABC refused to broadcast his *Andy Kaufman Special* (originally entitled *Andy's Fun House*). Acting as if he did not have any clue as to why the ABC executives did not accept the show, Kaufman insisted that there was nothing about the special that was "political or dirty" (Zehme 2001, 190). Along the same lines, Kaufman's manager, George Shapiro (in an interview for the television documentary *Biography: Andy Kaufman*), concedes that the said special "wasn't a comedy bit," but also points out that "it wasn't frivolous."

Both of these statements give some preliminary idea as to why Kaufman's comedy is radically different from Bruce's transgressive type. On a basic level, not only are hardly any of Kaufman's acts explicitly "political," but none of them is downright "dirty" either. Kaufman's performances are not rites of defilement in the sense of Kristeva's theory of abjection—which may be one reason why none of Limon's essays on stand-up comedians and the abject is devoted to Kaufman, who is not even mentioned in Limon's book. Unlike comedians like Lenny Bruce, Mel Brooks, and Richard Pryor, Andy Kaufman apparently does not support Limon's thesis that stand-up comedy is ultimately all about abjection.

On the other hand, if Lenny Bruce can be viewed as the exemplary "political" transgressor in comedy, then the question is to what extent the act of transgression is in fact still potent enough to constitute a radical cultural critique. Does not transgression belong to the aesthetic programs of modernist avant-gardes, and may it therefore not be the case that transgression as a political operation of critique has become obsolete in postmodern times? In fact, with the advent of postmodernism, the critical force of

In what seems like a parody of Lenny Bruce's law-invoking transgressions, Andy Kaufman stands trial in an imaginary courtroom. Accused of having "gone too far" in his show, he defies the judge and is subsequently "banned" from television. From *The Andy Kaufman Show* (Rhino Home Video, 1983).

transgressive acts has been repeatedly questioned by cultural theorists such as Fredric Jameson, Hal Foster, and Slavoj Žižek, who have denounced it as ineffectual within the cultural logic of capitalist hegemony. The central argument is roughly that any "radical" act of transgression is rendered pointless within the limitless domain of late capitalism, because it can never be anything other than an empty gesture. So how to deal with the theoretical specter that keeps haunting art practices in postmodern times, namely, the idea that the force of transgression has lost its potency as a strategy of subversion?

At this point, let me invoke Hal Foster as a paradigmatic example of a cultural theorist struggling to designate a new stance for critical art to operate in the era of postmodernism, when cultural practices are predominantly subject to the mechanisms of capitalist economy. Originally published in 1984 (a month before Andy Kaufman died), Foster's essay, "For a Concept of the Political in Contemporary Art," draws attention to the ways in which the very logic of capitalism effectively constitutes a deadlock for any form of radically political art in postmodern times.

As Foster forcefully points out, the impasse of transgressive art is that "the real radicality is always capital's, for it not only effects the new symbolic forms by which we live, but also destroys the old. More than any avant garde, capital is the agent of transgression and shock" (1984, 147). If capitalism truly produces its own ultimate force of transgression, then this entails that the notion of avant-garde as an aesthetics of transgression becomes obsolete, because the very idea of any cultural practice operating beyond existent border lines will always turn out to be already appropriated by capital. What this means for Foster is that the cultural logic of late capitalism is such that it calls for a "new positionality for political art" (152), and for artistic strategies that are alternative to transgression.

At the time of his writing, Foster was quite clear about what this other strategy should be. Since capital functions as the ultimate agent of transgression, Foster points out that what is required from art is an "immanent struggle" rather than "revolutionary transgression of social and cultural lines" (149). In other words, a space must be recovered where political art can operate as a critique from *within* postmodern culture, which implies that the transgressive politics of the avant-garde must be abandoned. If the "great beyond" no longer exists because the limitless domain of multinational capitalism has made transgressive gestures irrelevant, then political art must opt for a strategy that disrupts the cultural logic of late capitalism from within, a strategy that is "resistant" rather than transgressive, and it is this concept of "resistance" that Foster proposes as an alternative strategy for critical practices of art in late capitalism.

In what must be taken as both a theoretical proposition and a descriptive note on contemporary art, Foster explains what it means to engage in critical art practices according to a strategy of resistance, stating that "the political artist today [1984] might be urged not to represent given representations and generic forms but to investigate the processes and apparatuses which control them" (153). So the politics of this kind of "resistant art" would not exist in avant-gardist negotiations with, and challenges of, cultural and social limits, but its political stance would reside in the fact that "resistance" works strictly from within pregiven representational codes in order to question their ideological underpinnings.

Clearly, this specific essay from Hal Foster is not just mentioned here as a random example to illustrate the ways in which the transgressive aesthetics of the avant-garde have been challenged by postmodern cultural theorists. In *Presence and Resistance*, Philip Auslander uses Foster's concept of strategic resistance for

his analysis of Andy Kaufman's comedy as a mass-cultural entertainment version of conceptualist performance art. Drawing on
Foster's as well as Jameson's writings on critical art in postmodern
times, Auslander clearly aligns himself with the stance of these
theorists when stating his premise that political artists "must
interrogate the means of representation" in order to "expose the
ideological discourses that both define and mediate between images
and their audiences" (1992, 23). But then the question is, which
postmodern varieties of stand-up comedy would constitute acts of
resistance in Foster's sense, namely, as a critical investigation that
occurs within stand-up as a system of representation, questioning
the processes and apparatuses that control its codes?

In his brief historical outline of postmodernist forms of
stand-up comedy, Auslander distinguishes two main strands of
stand-up since the 1970s. The radical genre of "anticomedy"
emerged in the mid-1970s and was often used as a label for Kaufman's acts; this was followed by the backlash into nostalgia as
represented by the "club comedy boom," which was to become the
dominant form of stand-up in the 1980s (136). While the comedian of the latter type takes an essentially nostalgic stance, producing laughter that is complacent and pacifying, the structure
of "anticomedy" is radically self-reflexive and, consequently, the
laughter it elicits from its audience may be described as uncannily
hysterical, being a kind of laughter that is "unsure of its own
source and object" (137). Ultimately, the gesture of anticomedy
amounts to the performer's resignation of the conventional duties
that his or her "job" as a comedian entails.

If anticomedy takes as its subject the very "failure of comedy,"
on the part of the comic it constitutes some sort of melancholic
embrace—namely, an embrace of the condition that stand-up
comedy can no longer function as a "significant critical discourse"
in the cultural economy of postmodernism (137). Hence, one of

the central premises of anticomedy was to demask the codes of stand-up comedy as empty rhetoric. As the paradigmatic performer of anticomedy, Auslander invokes Steve Martin, arguing that "Martin's pastiche of comedy is void of content: his persona is blank and cynical, apparently only going through the motions of seeming to want the audience's attention and affection, treating the conventions of stand-up comedy as a *dead language*" (137, my italics). With the advent of anticomedy, comedy turned into its own obituary.

However, this emphasis on comedy as dead rhetoric was already noted at the heyday of the anticomedy movement. In a 1981 article in *Time* magazine, Richard Corliss coined an alternative term for what Auslander calls postmodern "anticomedy." Clearly referring to the same movement, Corliss wrote about the defiantly deviant variety of "anti-shtick," celebrating it as the harbinger of a "new wave" of comedians whom he subsumes under the category of the "Post-Funny School of Comedy" (86). Quoting Friedrich Nietzsche's famous aphorism that a "joke is an epitaph on an emotion," Corliss suggests that these post-funny comics produce "epitaphs on epitaphs," and ultimately, he argues, their performances are nothing less than a "requiem for popular entertainment" (87). According to Corliss, anticomedy was the genre of stand-up that announced the death of show business.

Clearly, this is nonsense. However "post-funny" the rhetoric of anticomics may have been, their acts were not so radically subversive as to constitute an ultimate refusal of comic entertainment. As Auslander notes, an exemplary anticomic like Steve Martin did question the codes of the genre, but he still made the audience laugh, so he "finally did fulfill the traditional imperatives of the comedian" (1992, 142). Finally, the question of the codes of traditional stand-up is exactly where Auslander locates the rupture embodied by Andy Kaufman. Though usually associated with the likes of self-reflexive anticomedians such as Steve Martin and Lily Tomlin, Kaufman's performance work marks a deviation from the self-conscious play with the imperatives of stand-up comedy as "dead rhetoric."[6] Kaufman, Auslander argues, cannot be neatly integrated into the category of postmodernist anticomedy because he ventures beyond the self-reflexive humor of an anticomic, mounting a more general "critique of postmodern culture" that exceeds the question of the conventional codes of "straight" comedy (138).

But if Auslander reads Kaufman's performance art as a critique of postmodern culture, what exactly does he mean by that? Reading Kaufman's performance art exclusively in terms of Foster's concept of "resistance," he argues that in his acts, Kaufman investigated and exposed the implicit ideological processes that are at work in the context of entertainment. Based on the work of theorists of postmodernist performance such as Chantal Pontbriand and Josette Féral, Auslander establishes the concept of "rejection of presence" as a potent critical strategy of performance art in order to deconstruct the "structures of authority within theatricality" and to expose "its ideological underpinnings" (44). In this sense, Kaufman's performance work functions as a series of critical acts of resistance which equally deconstructed the notions of aura and glamour:

> Kaufman's conceptual project was to put his own presence and authority as a performer radically at risk. More than any other performer working in the context of popular entertainment and more even than most working in avant-garde contexts, Kaufman undertook to deconstruct presence and discover strategies of resistance from within mass-cultural contexts. Kaufman investigated the context of stand-up comedy through a negative strategy similar to that of [Joseph] Kosuth and other conceptualist visual artists:

by refusing to fill the context of popular entertainment with the expected content. (140)

This argument about Kaufman's strategies of refusal is easily supported. Not surprisingly, Auslander invokes Kaufman's British Man character, who would do nothing but present a reading from F. Scott Fitzgerald's *The Great Gatsby* in front of his comedy club audience, starting from chapter 1.[7] As far as undermining the audience's expectations is concerned, this was clearly one of Kaufman's most notorious stunts, and Auslander is certainly right to state that this constituted a violation of "every expectation of what he, as a comic, was supposed to deliver" (140).

Incidentally, though, what Auslander misses here is that Kaufman's reading act later developed into a slightly more elaborate form when British Man made his appearance on *Saturday Night Live* and recited from *The Great Gatsby* on live television. As regards this particular reading, Bill Zehme and Bob Zmuda report that after futile negotiations with protesters from the audience in the studio, British Man finally agreed to play the musical record that he had planned to reward them with after they had patiently sat through his reading. And so British Man, in Zehme's words, "stalked over to the phonograph and set down the needle and waited through protracted hisses and skips until the sound of his voice issued forth" (2001, 208). Instead of the musical relief as presumably expected by the audience, the record turned out to be nothing more than the mechanically reproduced continuation of British Man's reading from *The Great Gatsby*. The difference was simply that instead of Kaufman's live voice, the machine was now doing the work, while British Man stood silently beside the phonograph.

This additional twist in the routine clearly reinforces Auslander's argument about Kaufman's "resistance of presence" even better than the plain comedy club version he invokes. For not only does Kaufman refuse to fill the context of *Saturday Night Live* with the expected content, delivering a high-culture literary reading instead of comedy entertainment, but more radically, Kaufman "punishes" the audience for having insisted on comedy, denying them the physical presence of his live voice.

Reading Kaufman's performance art not simply as a seminal redefinition of stand-up comedy, Auslander's highly evocative study certainly has its merits, as it offers a sophisticated analysis of Kaufman's work in terms of a critical interrogation of the codes of entertainment. Still, there are serious theoretical limitations to his perspective on Kaufman, and in order to test these limitations, I will briefly retrace another one of his points of argument.

As quoted above, Auslander sees Kaufman's negative strategy of refusal as bearing a significant resemblance to works of conceptualist artists like Joseph Kosuth. Indeed, he elegantly supports this thesis by showing that Kaufman's alleged similarity with Kosuth and the likes is valid for the formal characteristics of their artistic practices as well as the theoretical implications of these practices. Among other examples, he invokes what is probably the most notorious incident from the set of *Taxi*, the television sitcom that featured a version of Kaufman's Foreign Man as a comic stock character by the name of Latka Gravas. At one point, Kaufman successfully forced the producers to hire his lounge-singer character Tony Clifton as a separate actor for the series, so not only was Clifton granted a guest appearance on *Taxi*, but due to Kaufman's notoriously "fundamentalist" stance about not breaking character, it also involved that obscene Kaufman-as-Clifton would be present in the studio instead of cute Kaufman-as-Latka. When Kaufman-as-Clifton was fired off the set due to undisciplined behavior, he was literally dragged off the premises, while a journalist took photographs of the incident.[8]

At the time this incident took place, Auslander points out, the scene was nothing but a "private performance" witnessed only by those people who were present on the set, but subsequently, the incident "became well-known when accounts of it percolated into the media, to become the entertainment equivalent of a conceptual performance known to its audience only through documentation" (1992, 144). While this episode had all the bearings of a multilayered conceptual art performance, Auslander also admits to some limitations of the analogy between Andy Kaufman and the work of conceptual artists like Joseph Kosuth. Clearly, Kaufman did not adopt the "posture of avant-garde innovation" of Kosuth and the like; still, Auslander argues that Kaufman took even more radical risks "by allowing his work to be read as merely incompetent" (142).

Yet there is another, more fundamental limitation to Auslander's analogy between conceptual artists like Kosuth and Kaufman's performance work, and this consists in the fact that the cultural criticism enacted by Kaufman does not work according to the same political logic as the criticism represented by conceptual art. To test the politics of conceptual art, I will rely on Joseph Kosuth's essay "Art after Philosophy," which is not simply one of the seminal theoretical texts on conceptualism, but according to Hans Belting, nothing less than the "holy bible" for conceptual artists (1998, 460). In what is to be understood as one of his crucial slogans about conceptual art, Kosuth notes in "Art after Philosophy" that "a work of art is a kind of *proposition* presented within the context of art as a comment on art" (1969, 165, italics in original). Some lines further down, he elaborates on this idea, stating that a "work of art is a tautology in that it is a presentation of the artist's intention, that is, he is saying that a particular work of art is art, which means, is a *definition* of art" (165, italics in original). According to Kosuth, then, conceptual art refrains from providing any "positive" content to fill the institutional frame of art, denying the art market any object of presence. What the conceptual artist does instead is designate and investigate that very frame.

After some self-conscious hesitation, Kosuth finally provides what he calls the "purest" definition of conceptual art, pointing out that conceptualism is quite simply "an inquiry into the foundations of the concept 'art,' as it has come to mean" (171). What are the politics at work in aesthetic propositions like these? In *Das unsichtbare Meisterwerk* (The invisible masterpiece), Hans Belting concisely points out the anticapitalist thrust behind this theoretical stance of conceptualism, stating that the project of artists like Kosuth was primarily directed at a refusal to deliver a marketable work of art, because they would not subject to what they saw as a "capitalist abuse of art" (1998, 459, my translation). In this sense, conceptual art is certainly an exemplary strategy of resistance as put forth by Foster, because its critique functions internally to the system of the art market, and ultimately, the idea was that there would simply be no works of art to be appropriated by, and integrated into, the cultural economy of the capitalist market.

But finally, this is exactly why Auslander's analysis of Andy Kaufman is restricted in its perspective on Kaufman's performances as critical gestures within the entertainment business. Ultimately, the fact that he takes conceptual art and the notion of "rejection of presence" as his theoretical frame of reference makes for an interpretation that does not reach beyond the contextual constraints of art and theatricality. Reading Kaufman's acts as gestures that are confined within the institutional frame of their own context, Auslander disregards the possibility that Kaufman may have been not so much the conceptual artist of comedy, but a performer who questioned more than just the representational codes of comedy and entertainment.

Ultimately, then, the limitations of Auslander's analysis are correlative to the limitations of the politics of conceptual art. As Auslander aptly notes, the project of conceptualism was to question the context of art in order to investigate the "conditions and limits of that context largely by placing within it objects traditionally excluded from it" (1992, 140). This implies that, in the final instance, conceptual art is caught up in its own institutional frame, and its critical interrogation of representational codes remains a hermetical gesture concerned with nothing but its own trade. Consequently, an exclusive focus on Kaufman as conceptual artist weakens and obfuscates what may be the truly subversive edge of his performances. If Kaufman's critique of postmodern culture is reduced to a strategy of resistance that consists in radically undermining his own presence as a performer, his work is implicitly denied the potential to shatter ideological discourses on a broader cultural scale.

But what if Kaufman's strategy of political critique was neither that of avant-gardist transgression nor postmodernist resistance? In my reading of Kaufman, I propose a different focus that should reveal how the subversive impact of this apolitical, nontransgressive performer exceeded both common strategies of critical art: that of the "refusal of presence" as attributed to him by Philip Auslander, but also that of the heroically transgressive "comedy of abjection" as represented by Lenny Bruce and his postmodern successors.[9]

Overconformism as a Mode of Subversion

At the time Hal Foster wrote his essay "For a Concept of the Political in Contemporary Art," he proposed the shift of the positionality of critical art in terms of a transition from the modernist stance of avant-garde "transgression" to the postmodernist operation of immanent "resistance." More recently, Foster seems to have taken recourse to the concept of a transgression, for in his book *The Return of the Real* (1996), the notion of an avant-gardist aesthetics of transgression surfaces again. Here, one of Foster's theoretical enterprises is to counter a thesis from Jean Baudrillard, who has argued that the advent of multinational capitalism is in fact synonymous with an "end of subversion" within the domains of art and culture (quoted in Foster 1996, 128). According to Baudrillard, the works of pop art are unable to constitute radically political gestures of subversion because they are always already totally integrated into the political economy of commodity culture.

In his effort to recover the possibility of subversion, Foster opposes Baudrillard's stance, but he does not do so by recourse to his earlier notion of resistance. Instead, he returns to a revised conception of transgression, which is no longer to be thought in terms of avant-garde politics. Dismissing the "literal" notion of the avant-garde as some sort of troop crossing frontlines for a territory beyond existent cultural maps, Foster points out the option to "rethink transgression not as a rupture produced by a heroic avant-garde outside the symbolic order but as a fracture traced by a strategic avant-garde within the order" (157). In this way of thinking of the transgressive act as an internal fracture, Foster's position converges with the philosophy of Michel Foucault, to whose writings on transgression he is obviously indebted. If one of the pivotal points in Foucault's thinking is the insight that any resistance against a given power is always produced by the very power that it seeks to undermine, then transgression, accordingly, is also caught up in this reciprocal logic between a given order and the violation of its limits.[10]

Adopting Slavoj Žižek's theoretical reserves against Foucault's conception of subversion, I would argue that any force of transgression is always the product of the symbolic frame that it purports to undermine, and its "internal fractures" are preordained effects of that same discourse. Considering that every transgression is an immanent effect preproduced by the law, every transgressor effectively only sustains the discourse of power that he purports to rupture.[11] Ultimately, transgression functions as the necessary supplement to that same discourse, and in the context of comedy Lenny Bruce serves as the perfect example of how this works. Previously, I discussed Bruce in terms of his transgressive relation to the symbolic code, as a public performer who scandalously "recuperates" what must be excluded (or "abjected") in order for the law to constitute itself. In fact, what Lenny Bruce perfectly illustrates is not the supposedly subversive potential of transgression; on the contrary, he exemplifies the paradoxically affirmative relation that links transgression to the law. On account of this paradox, Slavoj Žižek has noted that

> it is not only that transgression relies on, presupposes, the Law it transgresses; rather, the reverse case is much more pertinent: Law itself relies on its inherent transgression, so that when we suspend this transgression, the Law itself disintegrates. (1997, 77)

Here, Žižek is clearly turning Foucault against Foucault, so to speak, and what this theoretical spin suggests for Lenny Bruce is that we may read this notoriously "outrageous" comedian precisely as an "inherent transgressor" who ultimately fails to redefine the symbolic field. As noted above, Bruce's transgressions ultimately function as a safeguard for the system of law that he purports to destabilize.

In terms of Lacanian psychoanalysis, the particular structure corresponding to transgression is that of perversion. As Žižek points out in *The Ticklish Subject*, the pervert is the exemplary agent of transgression insofar as he "brings to light, stages, practises the secret fantasies that sustain the predominant public discourse" (1999, 248). However, Žižek also makes it clear that such an act of staging fantasy before the public eye is not to be confused with an act of subversion, and in *The Plague of Fantasies* he articulates this paradox of the pervert's desire: "the pervert, this 'transgressor' *par excellence* who purports to violate all the rules of 'normal' and decent behaviour, effectively longs for the very rule of Law" (1997, 14, italics in original). In short, if the agent of perversion openly displays the unspeakable "dirty" fantasies that underlie the symbolic code, his aim is not to undermine the law, but to establish it and call upon its representatives to enforce it.

If this designates the workings of the pervert's true desire, then the frantic activity that Lenny Bruce would display on stage is strictly analogous to the structure of perversion. Forcing the law into action, even though this legal action should be brought against himself, Lenny Bruce turns out to be the pervert whose public acts of transgression ultimately serve only one function, namely, to bring the law into play in order make sure it is not "dead" yet. For the pervert, Slavoj Žižek points out, "*the object of his desire is Law itself*—the Law is the Ideal he is longing for, he wants to be fully acknowle[d]ged by the Law, integrated into its functioning" (14, italics in original). As Limon's reading has made clear, the same is true for Lenny Bruce. A public performer whose transgressive comedy constituted precisely such an appeal for acknowledgement on behalf of the law, Lenny Bruce is the paradigmatic example of what Žižek terms "inherent transgression."

Hence, if one were to perversely act out the secret fantasy scenarios that are locked away in the crypts of our culture, this enactment of what is forbidden would constitute nothing more than a transgression that is always already integrated into, and anticipated by, the unwritten law of the symbolic order. As Žižek notes, the symbolic order is not merely a container for the public

codes of law, but it refers to symbolic norms as well as the codi-
fied transgressions implied in these norms (1999, 264). This is the
reason why I would want to dismiss the concept of transgression
as based on a false radicality—even in Hal Foster's sense of an
"internal fracture" according to Foucault. Instead, I shall venture
for a different mode of critique, a strategy that may truly subvert
given ideological discourses, as its effects may be far more radically disconcerting than any force of transgression or any practice
of strategic resistance.

In an effort to counter the idea that the critique of ideology
is no longer possible in postmodern times, Žižek has put forth the
very compelling notion of subversion by means of an excessively
conformist rhetoric. Arguing that the ultimate threats to an ideological edifice are neither strategic acts of resistance from within,
nor outright perverse transgressions of its borders, Žižek has proposed that the truly subversive acts are those performed by subjects who strictly stick to the letter of the respective ideological
text. Accordingly, one of the central tasks of a postmodernist critique of ideology according to Žižek is "to designate the elements
within an existing social order which—in the guise of 'fiction,'
that is, of 'Utopian' narratives of possible but failed alternative
histories—point towards the system's antagonistic character, and
thus 'estrange' us to the self-evidence of its established identity"
(1994, 7). Thus, a subversion of ideological narratives is achieved
neither by means of transgressive acts nor by a strategy of resistance operating within the given ideological frame. For Žižek,
to critique an ideological discourse is to reveal its internal contradictions, and to point out the fundamental inconsistencies that
are occluded in the explicit ideological "text."

However, this strategy of estrangement is not to be confused
with the commonplace notion of "critical distance." As Žižek
makes clear, one of the forces of ideology lies in the paradox that

any imaginary distance toward an ideological discourse only confirms that the symbolic identification has been successful. Hence, he writes, "stepping out of (what we experience as) ideology is the very form of our enslavement to it" (1994, 6). This logic implies the possibility that the most potent strategy of radically undermining an ideological edifice might consist in gestures of absolute compliance with the symbolic identifications provided by that ideology. Maybe the most effective way to reach the point where we are estranged from the seemingly self-evident nature of ideology is to take the ideological text more literally than it is prepared (and "designed") to be taken, because it is in these gestures that the fundamental inconsistencies of any given ideology gain their full presence.

As Žižek points out in *The Plague of Fantasies*, the truly radical strategy of questioning an ideological discourse is not to "disregard the explicit letter of Law on behalf of the underlying fantasies, but to *stick to this letter against the fantasy which sustains it*" (1997, 29, italics in original). As a literary example for this strategy, Žižek invokes the protagonist from Jaroslav Hašek's celebrated novel *The Good Soldier Švejk*, a simpleton who "wreaks total havoc by simply executing the orders of his superiors in an overzealous and all-too-literal way" (22). A loyal subaltern whose obedience renders the military apparatus a farce, Švejk is an agent of subversion precisely because he has internalized the ideological discourse of the army in a fashion that is too literal. By taking the ideological apparatus more literally than it is prepared to be taken, the proverbial "good soldier" Švejk discloses the hidden cards of the discourse he identifies with and thus renders it inoperative. For this compelling notion of a mode of subversion that is grounded in an excessively literal symbolic identification with an ideological discourse, Žižek has coined the term *over-orthodoxy*, or overconformism.[12]

My thesis is that within the topography of American popular culture, Andy Kaufman may be read as precisely such an "overconformist author" whose performances constitute a radical critique of the symbolic identifications provided by the American Dream. As already pointed out, Kaufman's performance work shares hardly any correspondence with the strategy of transgression as represented by Lenny Bruce and the likes of what Limon calls "comedians of abjection." Unlike the pervert who voices those dark fantasies that must remain unspeakable, hidden, prohibited in the public discourse, Kaufman does not "break through" to any prohibited areas in order to display the obscene dirty undersides that are excluded from, and disavowed by, what we could call the public discourse of American culture. His strategy of critique will turn out to be far more uncanny.

In fact, Kaufman's uncanniness resides precisely in the fact that he does not transgress cultural limits. Strictly conforming to the terms of the symbolic codes of American culture, Kaufman is the faithful embodiment of that communal daydream that informs America's social imaginary. Hence, what ultimately sets him apart from Lenny Bruce is that he does not interfere with the symbolic order by bringing to light the "sick" fantasies that are disavowed, and prohibited by, the letter of the law. Instead, Kaufman enacts those presumably "healthy" fantasies that are already in the open for the public eye to see, and he stages those narratives of imaginary identifications that every American subject is supposed to live by—but he enacts these public fantasies in such a consistently literal way that their uncanny implications begin to show.

At this point, Jacques Lacan's concept of the "extimate" may prove helpful. According to the concise formula offered by Mladen Dolar, the Lacanian dimension of *extimité* is located "where the most intimate interiority coincides with the exterior and becomes threatening, provoking horror and anxiety. The extimate is simultaneously the intimate kernel and the foreign body" (1991, 6). Thus, Lacan's concept of the extimate marks that topological point where what we perceive to be the defining element of our innermost self-identity suddenly becomes something radically foreign, and what we presume to be the core of our subjectivity turns into an "other" that fundamentally unsettles our sense of self-consistency. This figure of thought provides yet another important theoretical hinge for my thesis, which relies on the idea that after all, what Andy Kaufman enacted on stage was perhaps not simply too weird for his contemporaries to "comprehend." On the contrary, the trouble may well have been that Kaufman's strange performances were too uncannily familiar in the context of American culture, because what Kaufman staged, however in an excessively literal way, was precisely the ideological core text that defines America's cultural identity.

The uncanny, Dolar points out in the same essay, is always at stake in discourses of ideology. After all, he writes, "ideology perhaps basically consists of a social attempt to integrate the uncanny, to make it bearable, to assign it a place" (19). With Andy Kaufman's excessively literal version of the American Dream, this social function of ideology to conceal the uncanny collapses as an effect of his sheer overidentification with the ideological letter. Ultimately, then, Andy Kaufman rendered visible the "extimate" dimension that lies at the core of what America perceives to be the element that constitutes, and lends consistency to, its cultural identity. In Žižek's terms, Kaufman will be shown to be the "overorthodox" performer in American entertainment business who gave away the "hidden cards," or inconsistencies and inherent paradoxes of the ideological edifice that is the American Dream.

Finally, when Richard Corliss, in his aforementioned essay on post-funny comedians, notes that humor is basically "detached analysis, an autopsy of the society's dreams and demons" (1981,

87), he implicitly offers an explanation as to why Andy Kaufman is no humorist, after all, and why comicality is not his mode of performance. Kaufman's performance art (or whatever you may want to call his work) is precisely not critically detached from the cultural topography that it questions. On the contrary, Kaufman's cultural criticism consists in the fact that he incarnates the very kernel of America's most potent ideology. Steve Allen probably comes closest to the true edge of subversion in Andy Kaufman when he compares him to a "religious fanatic," stating that everything he performs "is strangely real to him" (Corliss 1981, 87). In the last analysis, Kaufman will emerge as the truly fanatic member of the secular religious order that is the American Dream—the fundamentalist American dreamer.

The American Dream

.

The American Dream is that public fantasy which constitutes America's identity as a nation. But why is it appropriate to refer to this communal daydream as an ideological apparatus? Is it not just a set of social values and ideals that have long been drained of the actual meaning they may have had in the founding years of the United States? After all, one of the clichés about the American Dream today is that it has turned into a myth that is no longer adequate to the socioeconomic reality of present-day America. However, there is another, more ambiguous transformation that underlies this passage of the American Dream into an empty signifier. This is the passage whereby the "ideal" of the Dream is molded into "ideology."

In common usage, the American Dream is not understood in terms of an ideological discourse, and in the dictionaries it is still listed as an ideal that comprises a set of social values. In the *Oxford English Dictionary*, the "American dream" is broadly defined as the "ideal of a democratic and prosperous society which is the traditional aim of the American people," and as "a catch-phrase used to symbolize American social or material values in general." In the slightly more concise definition from the *American Heritage*

Dictionary of the English Language, the notions of "democracy" and "prosperity" are again closely connected to the concept of the American Dream, which is defined as an "American ideal of a happy and successful life to which all may aspire." In both of these general descriptions, the ideal of prosperity as represented in the American Dream figures as an emphatically *democratic* objective in the sense that it is open to each and every American subject.

Apart from this correspondence, though, the second definition involves a slight, but significant bend of the said principles. The emphasis from the strictly *societal* prosperity of the American nation is shifted toward the *personal* success and happiness of every single citizen or subject. Hence, according to the *American Heritage Dictionary*, the ideal trajectory delineated by the American Dream is not directed at a prosperous *society*, but it's the purpose of the American Dream to produce happy and successful individual *subjects*.[1]

Incidentally, this difference between the two definitions of the American Dream may be described in terms of their relation to the two foundational documents from American history. Focusing on democracy and prosperity as collective values of American society, the *Oxford English Dictionary* definition is correlative with those fundamental propositions written down in the Preamble of the U.S. Constitution, which is designed to promote "general Welfare" and the "Blessings of Liberty." Accordingly, the definition of the American Dream provided by the *American Heritage Dictionary* corresponds to the Jeffersonian emphasis in the Declaration of Independence, which says that "all men are created equal, that they are endowed by their Creator with certain unalienable Rights, that among these are Life, Liberty and the pursuit of Happiness." If the first definition of the American Dream is strictly correlative to the constitutional aim to organize the *totality* of the American people, the second reflects the insistence on the right to an autonomous "pursuit of happiness" of every *individual* as represented in the Declaration of Independence. Hence, the unwritten "ideal" which is the American Dream proves to be intricately rooted in the "soil" of the two foundational documents of the United States of America.

In its broadest terms as given by the dictionaries, the American Dream can therefore be interpreted as a paraphrase of those principles which the Preamble designates for the entire community of the United States. If one chooses to read it more narrowly (or naively) as an "ideal of a life full of happiness and success," an ideal that is "open to everyone," then the American Dream apparently articulates nothing more than the most basic of human rights according to the Declaration of Independence. In order to revalidate the concept of the American Dream as a productive theoretical tool in terms of its ideological force, this second, more "individualist" interpretation proves more appropriate as a starting point, because this definition exactly highlights the passage of the American Dream from "ideal" to "ideology."

After all, ideology is not just an ideal that comprises a set of social or material values, but rather, it is a discursive apparatus that "mediates" between a given ideal and the way it is reflected, or more precisely, *de*flected, in social reality. In his seminal article "Ideology and Ideological State Apparatuses," Louis Althusser offers a very concise definition of ideology as a representation of the "imaginary relationship of individuals to their real conditions of existence" (1970, 123). In this sense, ideology is a particular form of discourse in which the real antagonisms that pervade society are obfuscated, or reconciled in an imaginary form. Following Althusser, I would argue that the American Dream is an ideological apparatus precisely because it functions as an "imaginary representation" that bridges the gap between the symbolic "ideals" (such as those established in the said foundational documents) and the "real conditions of existence" in the United States of America.[2]

The notion of the American Dream as an ideal "to which all may aspire" provides a perfect example of the way in which ideology offers an imaginary correction of social antagonisms. "We are all made equal before the American Dream!" This insistence on the incorruptibly democratic structure of the Dream implies that if someone fails to lead a happy and successful life, it will be entirely the subject's own fault, not a result of social conditions that kept that person from fulfilling the promises of this ideal.

Initially, this insistence was not at all an ideological operation. In *American Civilization*, C. L. R. James has offered a provocative analysis of those ideals that are generally understood as the historical basis of the American Dream: namely, the notions of liberty, free individuality and the pursuit of happiness. By implication, he also provides an account of how these ideals have turned into ideology since the founding years of the United States of America. At that time, James points out, these ideals "had an actuality and a meaning in America which they had nowhere else" (1950, 31), and in the decades following the Declaration of Independence, social conditions were such that America presented a "spectacle of economic and social equality unknown in history" (40). As James points out further, it was only with the advent of modernism that American society became segregated by fundamental barriers.

These social barriers, James writes, reinforced the antagonisms of sex, race, and nationality, putting America in conflict with the ideals of its own founding charters: "The essential conflict is between these ideals, hopes, aspirations, needs, which are still the essential part of the tradition, and the economic and social realities of present-day America" (31). This is exactly where the American Dream presents itself as an ideological apparatus in Althusser's sense. After all, this public daydream purports to resolve the conflict addressed by James—and this is precisely what makes the American Dream an ideology, because it offers an imaginary resolution of the real social antagonisms that have come to pervade American society. Implicitly, the letter of the American Dream performs a negation or, rather, a correction of social differences.

However, this does not mean that ideology consists of an illusory simulation. As Slavoj Žižek points out in his essay on Althusser, ideology is no "malignant" apparatus designed to deceive us about the true state of things. Ideology, Žižek insists, "*has nothing to do with 'illusion,'* with a mistaken, distorted representation of its social content" (1994, 7, italics in original). An ideological apparatus is no more illusory (nor less real) than a fantasy—in fact, ideology functions according to the structure of fantasy. After all, the notion of fantasy does not refer to an imaginary space where one's desires, as in a hallucination, are realized, but it designates the very constituent of desire. In Žižek's concise formulation, fantasy is that which "constitutes our desire, provides its co-ordinates; that is, it literally 'teaches us how to desire'" (1997, 7). The American Dream works according to the very same logic. It is the public discourse that provides each American subject with the coordinates for his or her desire.

If every ideological discourse has the structure of a fantasy, there are methodological implications for any critical perspective on ideology. As I designate the American Dream as the foil for my reading of Andy Kaufman's performance art, my perspective is formed by Žižek's theoretical imperative that "an ideological text has to be read as a ciphered formation of the unconscious" (1997, 52). What does this mean exactly? First of all, this premise implies a structural analogy between ideologies and dreams. In strict analogy with Freud, Žižek points out that the unconscious wish and the latent dream-thought are not identical, but that "the unconscious wish articulates itself through the very distortion of the latent dream-thought" (52). Accordingly, this means that the fascination and the cultural impact of any ideological discourse is not to be found in the latent power structure that it conceals and modifies into a manifest text.

Instead, Žižek insists that the focus of any critique of ideology must be on the "economy of enjoyment" that underlies the ideological discourse (53). This also explains why, far from constituting some sort of "truth-effect," the pervert's violations of the symbolic code remain ultimately ineffective. As Žižek points out in *The Ticklish Subject*, that which surfaces in the ritual of perversion is not the Freudian unconscious—on the contrary, the perverse ritual makes it "drop out," because the unconscious is precisely

> *not* the secret phantasmic content, but something that intervenes *in between*, in the process of translation/transposition of the secret phantasmic content in to the text of the dream. . . . The Unconscious is that which, precisely, is *obfuscated* by the phantasmic scenarios the pervert is acting out: the pervert, with his certainty about what brings enjoyment, obfuscates the gap, the "burning question," the stumbling block, that "is" the core of the Unconscious. (1999, 247–48, italics in original)

Hence, the unconscious is no hidden "substantial" content that can be retrieved by perversely staging it in the open, but it consists in the "invisible" instance of censorship, the instance that codifies and filters that content.

If this is translated back into the terms of ideology as a "ciphered formation of the unconscious," it becomes clear that the crucial question is not what any given ideological discourse purports to promise, nor what latent thought is concealed beneath this ideological text. Rather, the focus of analysis must rest on the very process of censorship that translates one into the other. As far as Andy Kaufman is concerned, his deconstructive manipulation of the American Dream consisted in the fact that he did not even bother to manipulate it; as an overorthodox author, he took this public fantasy so literally that any explicit critique became unnecessary for its fundamental inconsistencies to be revealed.

But what is the discursive structure of this Dream, and in what way does it produce subjects of ideology? In his aforementioned essay, Louis Althusser put forth the idea that every ideological apparatus works according to an operation he terms *interpellation*. Taking the most ordinary of examples, Althusser invokes the everyday scene of an individual who is walking in the street and is hailed by a police officer; turning around, the individual acknowledges that he is the addressee of the interpellation, and "[b]y this mere one-hundred-and-eighty-degree physical conversion, he becomes a *subject*" (1970, 131, italics in original). Thus, individuals are "recruited" by an ideological apparatus. As Althusser suggests, it is this process of symbolic interpellation and subsequent recognition that transforms individuals into subjects of ideology. Reduced to its most basic structure, the interpellation of the American Dream entails nothing but the idea that in the proverbial "land of possibilities," we have the opportunity to *live the Dream*. Hence, if America hails us with the ideological promise that we can "live the Dream," we are only a subject of America in Althusser's sense as long as we accept ourselves as the addressees of this interpellation.[3]

Before breaking down the promise of this daydream into its constituents, let me briefly focus on the peculiar "economy of enjoyment" of this most basic form of the American dream ideology. If America stands for the opportunity to freely realize one's fantasies of a life of happiness, does this not make the American Dream very much a discourse of perversion according to Lacanian psychoanalysis? After all, this promise presupposes that "living the Dream" is what we actually want; therefore, this simple promise implies that to become American subjects (that is, to subject ourselves to the American Dream) is to be totally (perversely) certain that to realize our fantasies is what brings the greatest amount of happiness, and by implication, maximum enjoyment. Based on an absolute certainty as to what brings the most enjoyment, the American Dream clearly functions according to the logic of perverse desire. But if the structure of perversion curiously surfaces as the public ideological discourse, what does this tell us about the economy of enjoyment that underlies the American Dream?

The first thing to point out here is that in Lacanian theory, the notion of enjoyment does not refer to a state of spontaneous pleasure. As Žižek has noted, enjoyment is always "sustained by a superego imperative—as Lacan emphasized again and again, the ultimate content of the superego-injunction is 'Enjoy!'" (1997, 173). Hence, the supposed *promise* of enjoyment as issued by the most basic version of the American Dream implicitly translates into a universal injunction to act "perversely," that is, it amounts to nothing else than an actual *imperative* to enjoy the realization of our dreams. If "America" incorporates the opportunity that we *can* "live the Dream," what the rhetorical form conceals is that this promise is in fact an imperative: we *must* "live the Dream," because otherwise we would not qualify as American subjects.

Here we already have one of the structural problems with the American Dream. If America's ideological interpellation says, "live the Dream," this means that the (perverse) realization of our fantasies figures as the very letter of the law. Still, it would be wrong to assume that American culture is based on a collective fantasy that functions according to the logic of perversion. In fact, when perversion becomes universal, it is as in the epigram written on the sleeve of the Talking Heads album *Stop Making Sense* (1984): "When everything is worth money, then money is worth nothing." The same goes for the perverse structure of America's injunction to enjoy. After all, what is left of perversion if it is totally integrated into the public discourse and translated into the promise that everybody is free to act perversely?

Enjoy Your Serial Self!

In an essay entitled "American Pseudo," Frank Rich has ventured a most succinct formula of the American Dream on the basis of Tom Ripley as one of its most dazzling literary incarnations. In his reading of *The Talented Mr. Ripley* (1999), Anthony Minghella's Hollywood adaptation of Patricia Highsmith's novel of the same title, Rich argues that Ripley represents the democratic belief that "anyone can jettison the past, wipe the slate clean and with pluck and luck be whoever he or she wants to be" (1999, 81). For him, the most fascinating aspect about Ripley is the fact that he embodies the trouble and anxiety that is obfuscated in this supposedly "happy" version of this dream of self-invention. For the American Dream, Rich points out, is always haunted by its own "stealthy doppelgänger, the American tragedy that befalls the Gatsbyesque dreamer who goes too far" (81). What the character of Ripley illustrates is that even the successful enactment of the Dream necessarily implies a tragic dimension.[4]

Finally, Rich proposes a compelling formula to designate the basic structure of the American Dream. In his words, America's communal daydream consists in the belief that one can "find happiness by being someone else" (114). This axiom provides the basic coordinates for my account of the American Dream in terms of an ideological discourse. If we are "hailed" by the ideology of the Dream, the letter of the interpellation is this: *We can always remake ourselves for the sake of success and happiness.*[5]

In this sense, the American Dream functions according to two vectors. First, it reflects the "pursuit of happiness" as written in the Declaration of Independence, and in this respect, my definition based on Rich's formula converges with the definitions from the dictionaries mentioned above. Second, this trajectory of seeking "happiness" is based on the strategy of self-invention as the way to be successful in our "pursuit of happiness." Thus, the possibility to endlessly refashion our identity forms the additional element, which constitutes the second axis of the Dream.

Being strictly correlative to the right to pursue personal happiness, the first vector of the American Dream designates the imaginary objective of this communal fantasy. In other words, it provides the coordinates for our desire as a subject of the Dream. Implicitly, the first vector promises a successful and happy life, for it suggests that as long as we act like subjects interpellated by the American Dream, we "know" that happiness and prosperity are not a privilege of the few, but a *democratic* right for anyone who is willing to work for it. In short, the first vector of the Dream encompasses what is commonly referred to as the American "myth of success."

As Richard Dyer notes in his seminal study *Stars*, the myth of success generally implies that "American society is sufficiently open for anyone to get to the top, regardless of rank" (1998, 42). With this implication of upward mobility, the American Dream represents the ideological guarantee that no matter what one's previous history is, and regardless of social status, one can always "get ahead" in America. The proverbial "rags-to-riches" career is just the most extreme version of this myth of success, because it epitomizes the promise that all American subjects have equally the opportunity to promote their social and economic status. Hence, the first vector marks the American Dream as an ideological apparatus that purports that America functions like a *democracy of success*.

By extension, this vector also implies the promise that every subject of the American Dream has the opportunity to become a star. It may be safely assumed that the allure of stardom was not what Thomas Jefferson had in mind when he penned that phrase about the "pursuit of happiness," but in the final instance, stardom represents the mass-cultural equivalent of the traditional ideal of prosperity. After all, celebrities are those conspicuously "happy" subjects of the American Dream who have perfected the trajectory delineated by the myth of success. Stars are not only the very embodiment of success, but as semi-mythical individuals who are "loved by everyone," they also represent the prosperous subject *par excellence*. Ultimately, then, the American "democracy of success" is also a *democracy of stardom*.[6]

The second vector of the American Dream concerns the autonomy of the subject, and for the implications of this axis, let me return to Žižek's definition of fantasy. If the first vector of the Dream designates its imaginary objective and thus "provides the coordinates" for desire, then the second "teaches" its subjects "how to desire," that is, it tells how to proceed within the said coordinates of desire. This second vector provides the strategy to make sure we are successful on the pursuit of personal happiness, namely, it offers limitless possibilities of subject positions to be taken. This dimension of the American Dream grants complete freedom in the choice of who to be, which effectively turns into an imperative to "be whoever you want to be." Again, we are not simply offered (promised) an endless array of subject positions to be taken, but rather, what the ideological text of the American Dream imposes on us is the very desire to take the opportunity and "live" more than one subject position.

This is what makes the American Dream very much a fantasy scenario proper. As Jean Laplanche and Jean-Bertrand Pontalis state very concisely in their classic text on "Fantasy and the

Origins of Sexuality," the notion of fantasy is to be understood as the *setting*, or scene, of desire, not as a representation of its object (1964, 26). Explicitly referring to this particular passage from Laplanche and Pontalis, Judith Butler adds that strictly speaking, there is

> no subject who has a fantasy, but only a fantasy as the scene of the subject's fragmentation and dissimulation; fantasy enacts a splitting or fragmentation or, perhaps better put a multiplication or proliferation of identifications that puts the very locatability of identity into question. (2000, 492)

As the ideological text of the American Dream "recruits" its subjects with the promise that they may take any position within the cultural-geographical territory of the United States, this territory appears like a fantasmatic space in the strictly psychoanalytical sense of the word. As such, the second vector of the Dream is strictly correlative to the American frontier myth. Namely, once the vast space of the New World had reached its closure at the Pacific, and the geographical frontier could not be moved any further, the promises of a limitless domain were internalized and transformed into the promises of American subjectivity. Within the frame of fantasy offered by the American Dream, we may enjoy the vast space of our proliferation as a subject. Thus, the collective self-invention fantasy that is the American Dream appears like a blueprint for the very structure of fantasy itself— and to the extent that Andy Kaufman functions like a mirror of America's public fantasy, he assumes the position of the analyst within this setting.

The imperative of self-invention as issued by the Dream is a recurrent motif in American culture, and to illustrate the pervasiveness of this imperative, let me refer to Robert Jay Lifton's psychological study on what he terms *The Protean Self*. As Lifton outlines his argument at the beginning of his book, he points out that the process of "proteanism" is to be understood as the continuous mental re-creation of one's own sense of self. Thus, it becomes clear that his notion of the "protean self" is strictly correlative to the self-invention imperative of the American Dream. What is important to note, though, is that for Lifton, the fluidity and multiplicity implied in this potentially endless procedure of refashioning one's self does not entail that the self disappears or loses any sense of coherence. On the contrary, the protean process according to Lifton "involves a quest for authenticity and meaning, a form-seeking assertion of self" (1993, 9). Eager to dispel anything that may sound vaguely "postmodernist" about his tribute to proteanism, Lifton emphatically insists on the *agency* of self-making. As protean subjects, it seems that we are not embedded in any discourses of power, but we just keep reinventing ourselves on our own.[7]

Clearly, Lifton does not explicitly invoke the American Dream as the ideological discourse that informs his perspective, but then *The Protean Self* features a chapter entitled "America, the Protean Nation." In this section, Lifton points out that America designates that particular cultural frame where the process of proteanism is integrated into the symbolic network as a mode that is essential to its functioning. His argument is that Americans see themselves as essentially a "people of metamorphosis," and he ends this chapter on the "Protean Nation" with the remarkable conclusion that "such is our history that we have never been other than protean" (32, 49). Considering Lifton's strongly affirmative and optimistic perspective on the process of proteanism, it becomes clear that in the final instance, his position is that of a fervent advocate of the injunction to reinvent yourself as issued by the American Dream.[8] Finally, when Lifton notes that "America's proteanism . . . is inseparable from the nation's status as a *land of promise*" (41, my italics), he even delivers the key phrase, which brings us back to the manifest text of the American Dream.

After all, what remains to be shown is that the very structure of the American Dream is such that its promises are permanently suspended. This has to do with the peculiar "economy of enjoyment" that underlies this ideological discourse, with its two vectors of (1) finding happiness by means of (2) reinventing oneself. The first thing to note is that in Lacanian psychoanalysis, the notion of enjoyment (*jouissance*) is not to be confused with the Freudian concept of the "pleasure principle." In Žižek's words, the term *jouissance* refers to the unbearably painful, even "lethal" excess of enjoyment which threatens "to draw us into a psychotic night" (1997, 184). Hence, the subject desperately tries to maintain a distance from this traumatic enjoyment, and in the symbolic order, this distance is safeguarded by the rule of the pleasure principle. As Dylan Evans points out, the Freudian pleasure principle functions as a "law which commands the subject 'to enjoy as little as possible'" (2001, 91). As the subject keeps trying to transgress this law that blocks him from enjoyment, the pleasure principle effectively amounts to nothing other than an actual prohibition of what Lacan terms *jouissance*.[9]

Considering that the American Dream as designated above does not impose any prohibition of enjoyment upon its subjects, it apparently functions according to a strangely inverted logic of *jouissance*. It may seem that, ultimately, America's structurally perverse promise that one can "live the dream" of success amounts to nothing less than a dictate to enjoy as much as possible, so its economy of enjoyment seems curiously at odds with that of the symbolic order as outlined above. Not only does the American Dream *not* prohibit enjoyment, but in its ideological text, it seems that the prohibition is translated into an obscene injunction that purports that *jouissance* is in fact accessible for everyone. Still, the American Dream works perfectly well as a safeguard against that traumatic excess of enjoyment that Lacan terms *jouissance*. This is because the promise to "live the Dream" and enjoy functions according to an inverted logic of repression. If enjoyment is not only *not* prohibited, but actively endorsed by the predominant public discourse, the result of this injunction is that it effectively keeps at bay the very enjoyment that it explicitly encourages us to seek.[10]

More important, though, the process of limitless self-invention necessarily fails to put the subject in any position to enjoy, and the path to happiness as designated by the American Dream is bound to miss its destination. Why is this? The ideological letter of the Dream purports that every American subject is entitled to his or her pursuit of happiness. It even encourages us to embrace enjoyment, but in doing so, the American Dream commits us to a frantic activity of self-making which effectively functions as the stumbling block for what it offers. Mark Seltzer, in his study on *Serial Killers*, offers a succinct formulation of this peculiar problem when he argues that "the self-made subject is subjected to an endless drill in self-making that becomes indistinguishable from a repeated self-evacuation" (1998, 116). This "drill" of self-invention constitutes one of the fundamental inconsistencies of the American Dream, for it ensures that the ideological promise of enjoyment remains suspended in a double bind, and thus prevents the fulfillment of this promise.

By literally enacting the public fantasy that is the American Dream, Andy Kaufman stages the internal contradictions of its injunction to reinvent ourselves for the sake of success and happiness. On the one hand, Kaufman acts as the "nice" American star who has perfected the trajectory prescribed by the myth of success and enjoys the love of his fans, but at the same time, he confronts his audiences with the "psychotic night" of excessive enjoyment,

which he draws from his limitless proliferation of identities—
and in his literal-minded devotion to this drill of self-invention,
he reveals that this enjoyment can only be gained at the expense
of your own self-evacuation. In this sense, Andy Kaufman represents the uncanny "incarnation" of this traumatic *jouissance* that
forms the unacknowledged kernel of the American Dream.[11]

How I Learned to Stop Worrying and Avoid Dead Ends

Finally, if an ideological text is to be regarded as a "ciphered formation of the unconscious," then what is the process of censorship at work in the public fantasy that is the American Dream?
In Renata Salecl's concise formulation, fantasy is defined as the
way in which "the subject organizes her or his enjoyment around
some element of trauma" (1994, 87). In Freudian psychoanalysis,
the notion of trauma is usually associated with castration, but in
an effort to transcend the sexual encodings of Freud's concept of
castration, I would suggest that every form of traumatic knowledge is a corollary of a recognition of mortality.[12] Accordingly, the
public fantasy that is the American Dream constitutes an orga-
nizing principle of enjoyment that functions as a safeguard against
the traumatic recognition of one's mortality. In short, the American Dream is a protective fiction against our knowledge of the
contingency of death.

Now, what makes the American Dream so attractive as an
ideological discourse is the way this traumatic knowledge is integrated into its very structure as a myth of success. As happiness
and prosperity figure as the imaginary objectives of the American
Dream, the trajectory delineated by this public fantasy is ultimately directed at some sort of "social immortality." After all, if
the ideological interpellation of the American Dream produces
subjects who believe in America as a "democracy of success," then
the epitome of such social and economic advancement is the

immortal star. Having successfully secured themselves a place in the collective memory, stars are immortal to the extent that they outlive themselves in their own image, as cultural icons. Hence, if the first vector of the Dream designates the coordinates of desire and purports that America is also a "democracy of stardom," its ideological function is that it offers a promise to circumvent mortality, or more precisely, it provides an escape from the traumatic finality of death.

But what if we fail on this trajectory toward gaining the status of an immortal cultural icon? Then there is always the "safety net" provided by the second vector of the American Dream. In case we find ourselves stuck in a dead end, having failed to immortalize ourselves by means of stardom, we are offered an infinite number of possible exits, because as a true subject of the Dream, we can always become someone else, refashion the representation of our self and "wipe the slate clean" in order to start another effort to enact the American myth of success. Thus, the structure of the American Dream is such that it offers a dual strategy to evade death.

In Robert Jay Lifton's concept of the "protean self," if the notion of proteanism designates the process of continuously reshaping one's identity, then Lifton claims this process is a quintessentially American structure, and in one of his most revealing arguments, he states that proteanism "provides a capacity to *avoid dead ends*" (1993, 11, my italics). In a very literal sense, what Lifton articulates here is nothing else than the bottom line of the promises offered by the American Dream. Ultimately, what the Dream ideology purports is that America is the place where we get the opportunity to defer our own death—first of all because of the "democracy of stardom" implied in the myth of success, and second because the very structure of the American Dream implies a guarantee of interminability. America is where a subject can become immortal, not only because fame is supposedly free and available to everyone, but also because it allows the creation of ever-new representations of one's self. Even if we are denied access to the symbolic immortality provided by stardom, we can always free ourselves from this "dead end" by producing a new, more successful version of our self in order to start again on the endeavor to turn into a cultural icon.

Hence, the traumatic recognition of mortality functions as the inherent stain of the American Dream, which needs to be precluded for the ideology to remain operative. In the final instance, the American Dream constitutes a protective fantasy that organizes the desire of its subjects around the traumatic void of death, and because it does so by means of an injunction to reinvent oneself, it invariably produces subjects of hysteria. After all, the clinical structure of hysteria designates the continuous process of producing a multiplicity of self-fashionings, a process that serves as a protective strategy against the traumatic recognition of mortality. Referring to Freud's early studies of hysteria, Elisabeth Bronfen has pointed out that the hysteric "seeks interminability" in the face of trauma (1998, 32). The hysterical subject not only "overwrites" the traumatic stain of mortality by means of a seemingly limitless array of personae, but her performance also implies a recognition of the very thing it is designed to dissolve, namely, the knowledge of death.

In its basic mode, the American Dream works according to the very same structure, the central analogy with hysteria being that the dream-ideology shields its subjects from the traumatic void of death by means of a promise that grants the possibility of multiple self-fashionings. Clearly, though, the American Dream represents a version of hysteria that is both pacified in its structure and pacifying in its effect. After all, the recognition of mortality is totally eclipsed, as it were, by its ideological injunction to remake oneself, and by the promise of immortality implied in the "democracy of stardom." If the hysteric persistently communicates a knowledge about the traumatic void of death, this recognition of radical negativity is displaced in the ideological apparatus that is the American Dream. While the subject of hysteria "seeks interminability," the interpellation of the American Dream produces subjects who serially reproduce themselves in the cause of success, happiness, and the symbolic "immortality" that resides in stardom.

If the traumatic knowledge of mortality is eclipsed in the letter of the American Dream, this repressed knowledge returns in the performance work of the fundamentalist American Dreamer. Taking this public fantasy by its word, Andy Kaufman articulates how death functions as the central stain or void within the ideology of the American Dream.

CHAPTER 3

The Postmodern Escape Artist

Je est un autre.

> —Arthur Rimbaud

Andy Kaufman is me. I'm Andy Kaufman.

> —Andy Kaufman

In their comments on their shooting script for Milos Forman's biopic *Man on the Moon* (1999), screenwriters Scott Alexander and Larry Karaszewski report two significant crises that occurred during the process of adapting Andy Kaufman's biography for the screen. Both of these problems concern the precarious seriality of selves that Kaufman enacted in the course of his entertainment career.

The first crisis surfaced before Alexander and Karaszewski actually started writing, and it has all the bearings of an avant-garde event in Hal Foster's sense of a "failure to signify." The trouble was that the writers were unable to discern any pattern underlying the series of events that constituted Andy Kaufman's performance work—a pattern that would function as an ordering principle for the narrative of the film. With so many moments in Andy Kaufman's life being "bogus," as they put it, they were initially bewildered as to the significance of what they considered "fake events." And what is even more devastating for screenwriters of a Hollywood biopic, they simply "didn't see a narrative" (vii). Clearly, Alexander and Karaszewski's problem was the supposed lack of structure in Kaufman's body of work, as his career appeared too incoherent and too contingent for them to see how this confusing tangle of seemingly senseless and unconnected events should be translated into a meaningful narrative sequence.

The second crisis proved even more serious, and despite the fact that it surfaced belatedly, this second problem was possibly what had caused the preceding problem in the first place. While already busy conceiving the narrative, the writers faced what was basically a problem of characterization when they suddenly realized that "something was off. We didn't know what the movie was about. We didn't know who Andy was. Panic set in. The thousands of anecdotes weren't coalescing into a character, a guy whom we understood. Andy was just a cipher moving through a series of episodes—our greatest fear" (xi). At one stage or another, every screenwriter is probably seized by this kind of panic, but this particular crisis is crucial with regard to Andy Kaufman. What the writers felt was missing in their script was a full subjective presence that, quite simply, made sense; there was no subject present, only a vacant entity by the name of Kaufman, an incoherent character who was nothing but an empty vessel that did not contain any meaning in itself.

In order to correct this, Alexander and Karaszewski kept searching their notes for some sort of key that would help them decipher the "cipher" that was Andy Kaufman and thus lend consistency to Kaufman's biography as an entertainer. Implicitly referring to Orson Welles's classic *Citizen Kane* (1941), they would call this key their "Rosebud" (xi), meaning a master signifier that would unlock the enigma of Kaufman in a way similar to the childhood memory that lends closure to the fictional biography of Charles Foster Kane in *Citizen Kane*. As soon as such a Rosebud would be found among the biographical particles, the problem of narrative coherence would vanish along with the persistent mysteries surrounding Kaufman. After all, if the enigma of his "true self" might be explained by way of a defining key element, then the writers would be able to translate Kaufman's career into a narrative sequence in which the episodes would be linked according to the most basic convention of the biopic genre—everything that may seem contingent and incoherent about someone's life would be transformed into a biographical trajectory that appears to be ordered by a principle of necessity.

The writers of *Man on the Moon* could not find any Rosebud, but they were smart enough to turn this aspect into the most outstanding quality about their screenplay.[1] Unlike the standard Hollywood biopic, *Man on the Moon* does not present the protagonist in such a way as to encapsulate some imaginary kernel of his personal identity. Instead of filling the central void constituted by Kaufman's endlessly dissimulated selves, Alexander and Karaszewski came up with a figure of thought that may seem like the most banal simile for this kind of deferral. In order to solve their problems with making Kaufman a meaningful presence in their screenplay, they decided that their protagonist should be "like an onion—layers of masks and subterfuge. But when you peeled off the final layer, trying to get a look at the man inside, there was nothing there. It was anti-Rosebud, and conceptually perfect" (xii).

This poetological strategy provides the momentum for Forman's film, and it is explicitly articulated in the scene where Kaufman's girlfriend, Lynne Margulies (played by Courtney Love), tells Andy that "there *is* no real you" (118, italics in original). As far as biopics are concerned, *Man on the Moon* undermines the genre to the extent that it does not rely on essentialist notions of identity, since the protagonist is depicted as nothing but a series of displaced identities.

However, Alexander and Karaszewski are missing something in their self-celebratory account of how they avoided the standard Hollywood practice to lend closure to their protagonist. What the

screenwriters fail to see is that their conceptual twist to "not capture the essence" of Andy Kaufman contains a theoretical punchline that undermines their own structural spin. The very concept
of "anti-Rosebud" constitutes yet another master signifier that
every aspect about Kaufman may be related to. While it purports
to bear witness to the inaccessible kernel of Kaufman's identity,
the idea of "anti-Rosebud" actually masks the neat and easy "poststructuralist" strategy to declare that the central absence is itself
the kernel. In a way, then, the solution as offered by Alexander and
Karaszewski consists of a mere rhetorical trick: if the essence
of something is too elusive, just declare that the absence of the
essence is in fact the essence. Strictly speaking, this position is
not anti-essentialist because it presupposes the notion of essence.
Ultimately, then, the concept of "anti-Rosebud" is no more than
yet another Rosebud, though one that is defined *ex negativo*. As
biographical narratives go, the screenplay for *Man on the Moon*
may seem like a poststructuralist take on *Citizen Kane*, but in fact,
it is based on an excuse in the guise of a postmodern theory of
subjectivity.[2]

Still, these practical problems reported by the screenwriters
do have some theoretical value. They convey a preliminary idea
of the way in which the postmodernist thesis of the effacement of
the subject pertains to Andy Kaufman. If the notion of a consistent, self-centered subject was the most potent myth of en-
lightened modernism to be shattered in postmodern times, then
Kaufman enacted this dissolution in a most radical way. Arguably,
the uncanny implications of the notion of the decentered subject
of postmodernism have never been more prevalent in popular
entertainment than in Kaufman's performances—in fact, he may
perfectly be described as a *postmodern escape artist* in terms of
subjectivity. If the stunt of traditional escape artists like Harry
Houdini was to change the whereabouts of the body and free

the artist from physical restraints, Kaufman's acts were escapes in terms of his self, while physically, he usually remained in one place.[3]

If Andy Kaufman, as an entertainer, enacts the postmodern thesis about the absent kernel of the subject, let me briefly consider a literary figure that makes for one of the most fascinating illustrations of this "vacant subject" of postmodernism. In a way, Kaufman shows a somewhat surprising structural correspondence to one of the more gruesome literary incarnations of the "dead" subject of postmodernity, namely, the protagonist from Bret Easton Ellis's infamous novel *American Psycho* (1991). Undoubtedly the most scandalous piece of American literature of the 1990s, this textual monstrosity of a novel is centered around Patrick Bateman, a Wall Street executive who may also be a serial killer, though the text remains ambiguous about the question of the dead bodies produced by Bateman being real or figments of his imagination.

Regarding the logic of subjectivity that is at stake in *American Psycho*, one crucial passage toward the end of the novel shows Bateman, who functions as the narrator-focalizer in the book, explicitly theorizing his own status as a subject. Exhausted by the violent excess of his noctural alter ego, he states that "there is an idea of a Patrick Bateman, some kind of abstraction, but there is no real me, only an entity, something illusory" (376). Just a few lines further down, Bateman reaches the final verdict on his self, discarding the myth of a coherent subject for good: "*I simply am not there*. It is hard for me to make sense on any given level" (377, italics in original). The latter part of this quote from *American Psycho* sounds like a distant echo of Kaufman's "failure to signify," as discussed above. As far as his contemporaries were concerned, Kaufman, too, did not make sense "on any given level."

Beyond this somewhat trivial analogy, Bateman's perspective on his own self proves to be perfectly compatible with the vacant entity that is Andy Kaufman as portrayed in *Man on the Moon*. In fact, Bateman's words may very well serve as some sort of shorthand formula for what was at stake in Kaufman's performances of the dissolution of his self. Just like (imaginary or real) serial killer Patrick Bateman, "serial subject" Kaufman is also "simply not there" in the sense that there is no coherent self present about which we might positively say "what it is," or topologically speaking, "where it is." If there is only "an idea of a Patrick Bateman," but no "real" him, the same is true for Andy Kaufman, and even more radically so. To be more precise, Kaufman produces some sort of short-circuit between the two crucial functions in Bateman's account on his self. With Kaufman, it is not that there is only an idea of him, but no real self behind his masks of identity. Rather, these two functions are linked in a relation of interdependence, for the idea of Andy Kaufman is that "there is no real Andy Kaufman"—or conversely, the fact that there is no real Andy Kaufman amounts to the very idea that (according to *Man on the Moon*) "is" Andy Kaufman.[4]

Yet this perspective was not at all new at the time Alexander and Karaszewski wrote their anti-Rosebud screenplay, nor did their poststructuralist stance mark a deviation from what was already the standard interpretation of Andy Kaufman. *Man on the Moon* simply marks the event that fixed this apparent absence of any "real" Andy in a consistent cinematic after-image. Long before Forman's film went into production, Kaufman had been recognized as the performer who epitomized the postmodern idea of the "death of the subject" in the context of popular entertainment. Almost a decade before the release of Forman's biopic, Philip Auslander had argued that in the last consequence, "there is no real Kaufman, only a series of displacements without final referent" (1992, 151). If Karaszewski and Alexander had read Auslander before writing *Man on the Moon*, they might as well have spared themselves the trouble of looking for a master signifier for their fictional re-creation of Kaufman.

Clearly, Auslander's analysis was one of the first studies to consistently theorize the common place about the absence of any "real" Kaufman. As mentioned above, Auslander drew on an earlier article by Michael Nash, who had already offered a similar argument about Kaufman as displaced subject—yet with a significant additional point regarding the way this affected Kaufman's career commercially. As Nash argues, it was precisely this lack of referential closure in Kaufman's play of identities that provoked discomfort among television executives at ABC when they were faced with Kaufman's special *Andy's Funhouse* (1977). According to Nash, one spokesperson from the network complained that the trouble was that "you can't tell which one is the real Kaufman" (1990, 7). So it seems that ultimately, this complete absence of any "final referent" was far more unsettling than the rather trivial fact that *Andy's Funhouse* was not a traditional comedy special, bearing the potential to redefine the format. What seemed to disturb the executive board was not the fact that this special was too "offbeat" in the sense that it did not conform to the codes of the genre— what troubled them was the sheer "invisibility" of the performer who, though he was physically present throughout, appeared to vanish among the mirrorings of his self-representations.

At any rate, ABC refused to air *Andy's Funhouse*, and so did NBC later on. On August 28, 1979, after the tape had been stored on the shelves for two years, ABC finally aired it under the new title *The Andy Kaufman Special*. In the meantime, Kaufman had turned into beloved Latka on *Taxi*, but when Janet Maslin reviewed the show for the *New York Times*, her remarks on Kaufman's "comic elusiveness" reflected some of the same concerns expressed previously by the executives at ABC: "When any of the several characters Mr. Kaufman impersonates here suddenly proclaims himself 'the real me,' rest assured that he is lying" (quoted by Zehme 2001, 191). But once again, the very notion of lying presupposes that there is a true self that can be masked behind a lie in the first place. However, the crucial point is that during his entire performance career, Kaufman never showed any "substantial" essence of self that any one of his self-fashionings could legitimately lie about. In an attempt to offer some sort of a genealogy of these personae, I am going to show how the entertainer that was Andy Kaufman came to be truly and originally displaced to such a degree that his characters literally had a life of their own from the very start.

The Mask Is the Face Is the Mask

The question is, where and how did this series of displacements of Kaufman's identity begin, and what is the actual performance material that produced this popular cliché that "there is no real Andy" in the first place? How did Kaufman enact the disappearance of himself as a subject, and to what extent is his dissimulation

"Here I come to save the day." Jim Carrey's reenactment of Andy Kaufman's Foreign Man act on the premiere of *Saturday Night Live*. From *Man on the Moon* (Universal Pictures, 1999).

of selves strictly correlative to the ideological edifice that is the American Dream?

Clearly, any effort to pin down the exact point in history when Andy Kaufman entered popular consciousness is always a construct from a belated point of view (and thus, another Rosebud). As with every historical origin, this primary impact on the American public can never be established any other way than by a retroactive gesture, but with Kaufman, this "primordial scene" clearly coincides with the premiere of NBC's comedy show *Saturday Night Live* on October 11, 1975. In terms of television history, Kaufman made his national debut the year before, when he appeared on *The Dean Martin Comedy World*, but his first large-scale impact on America came with his guest appearance on the very first segment of *Saturday Night*, as it was then called.[5] In the character of Foreign Man, Kaufman entered the stage in order to do nothing but lip-synch the chorus from the *Mighty Mouse* theme song. In *Man on the Moon*, Jim Carrey offers a dazzling re-enactment of this scene from *Saturday Night*, and Bob Zmuda, in his book *Andy Kaufman Revealed!*, recounts this original Foreign Man act as follows:

> Following the opening sketches, Andy stepped out into a lone spotlight, smiled, set the tone arm of a small phonograph onto a record, and a scratchy rendition of the theme song from the *Mighty Mouse* cartoon series began. Saying nothing, he bobbed along the music until the refrain *"Here I come to save the day!"* which, while flourishing his hands, he lip-synched. He then fell mute until it appeared again. When the song finished, he removed the tone arm and bowed. (Zmuda and Hansen 2001, 59, italics in original)[6]

What is crucial about the way Kaufman made his national debut on *Saturday Night* is that this "primordial scene" is, in fact, strictly complicit with one the most basic mythical narratives implied in the American Dream. On a basic level, Kaufman's act may be read as a desperate attempt to adapt to America by way of mimickry, lip-synching the heroic chorus "Here I come to save the day" from the *Mighty Mouse* theme song. Yet what is even more significant about this act is the fact that when Kaufman first introduced himself on national television, he did so in the persona of Foreign Man. Entering America's popular consciousness as Foreign Man, he basically re-enacts the most fundamental myth about America as the land of opportunities where immigrants can reinvent themselves and start a "new life." Thus, Andy Kaufman's debut on national television not just quotes, but effectively stages, the "primal version" of the narrative of promise that is the American Dream.

At the time Kaufman made his debut on the first segment of *Saturday Night*, this representational ambivalence that made it difficult to tell the performer from the character already existed. As Bill Zehme points out, it seemed as if Kaufman had "materialized from nowhere, inexplicably, like a wraith" (2001, 152). Likewise, Kaufman's manager, George Shapiro, recalls in the television documentary *Biography: Andy Kaufman* (1999) that the impact of Kaufman's performance as an immigrant from the imaginary island of Caspiar was such that "every one in America thought he was a foreign person." When Andy Kaufman entered American popular culture on a national scale, he was literally dis-placed from the very beginning.

At the start of his career in the entertainment business, Kaufman was therefore always already "out of place" in a double sense. On a basic level of performance, he presented himself as the proverbial Eurasian immigrant who had left his home country for the land of possibilities in order to become a show-business star, no matter what his talents were. But on a more fundamental level, that is, in terms of the relation between his own self and his stage personae, Kaufman was already "beside himself" when he introduced himself on television as Foreign Man. This is to say that America has never experienced Andy Kaufman "pure and simple," because at the time of his debut, any supposedly "real" Andy was already literally dis-placed, and irretrievably lost in his own altered identities.

In some sense, this brings me back to the notion of abjection, which Julia Kristeva defines as an experience of ecstasy in a very literal sense. Right at the beginning of her seminal work *Powers of Horror,* she writes about the one who is "haunted" by the "spasm" of abjection, arguing that he is positioned "literally besides himself" (1982, 1). Clearly, this figure of ecstasy presupposes that there is in fact a place where the subject is *not* beside himself, but self-identical, within his own self. This is precisely not the case with Andy Kaufman, who can never be "literally beside himself" because strictly speaking, he has never been "with" himself, either. In other words, the topology of ecstasy as a theoretical figure does not apply to Kaufman because his subjective condition is, and has always been, permanent ecstasy. Within the topography of American popular culture, Kaufman truly represents the always already (originally) decentered subject, whose self was deferred from the very start of his professional performing career.[7]

Among the various personae that Kaufman would create during his career, Foreign Man was clearly the most popular of all. As Philip Auslander points out, though, once it had become "common knowledge that the Foreign Man was a fictional creation of Kaufman's, that performance lost most of its impact and was ripe for translation into an endearing character on a popular situation comedy" (1992, 143). This was Latka Gravas from the television series *Taxi*, which began production in 1978. Thus, having started out as a character who was truly displaced in more than one sense,

Foreign Man was transformed into a sitcom character whose displacement merely consisted in the fact that his fictional biography implied that he was of foreign origin. While Kaufman's early Foreign Man acts were suspended on the borderline between fiction and reality, this was no longer the case within the context of situation comedy. Accordingly, Latka's representational status never came close to the precarious ambiguity of his previous incarnation by the name of Foreign Man.

Kaufman's own status as an entertainer grew more precarious when he created his Tony Clifton character. A rude and musically inept Las Vegas lounge singer, Tony Clifton dressed in excessively tacky suits, wore sunglasses, a large moustache, and a wig that was clearly not supposed to look like anything other than

An uncomfortable by-product of the American Dream and an obscene incarnation of its recurring failure: Tony Clifton in *The Midnight Special* (Sony Music Entertainment, 1981).

a wig. On the whole, Clifton's appearance seemed too much like the effort of a makeup artist (which it was) for Clifton not to be regarded as a travesty—and this excess of markers of parody is what sets him apart from the pretense of authenticity displayed by Foreign Man's "unmasked" straight-face.

Still, the two are analogous to the degree that they both are clearly discernable as representations of "proverbial" American identities. While Foreign Man represents the "original myth" of the immigrant who enters the land to test the promises of the American Dream, Tony Clifton is of Las Vegas origin, which means that he surfaced from that mirage-like city in the Western desert which harbors the "heart" of the American Dream—Las Vegas being that geographical place in America's cultural landscape where re-creations of the self and glamorous prosperity are celebrated in a most excessive fashion.[8] As such, Clifton is already a result of the ideological promises implied in the American Dream. While Foreign Man represents the "naive" believer of this ideological discourse, Clifton is more like an uncomfortable, disagreeable by-product of America's public fantasy. He is the miserable figure of the never-quite-risen star, neither promising icon of the future, nor has-been—in short, Clifton is an incarnation of the recurrent failure of the American Dream, and now he seems to take revenge on his audience by acting as a public nuisance.

While charmingly inept Foreign Man hardly ever caused any kind of irritation, Tony Clifton often provoked discomfort, even outrage, as Andy Kaufman strictly refused to let the mask of his stage persona slip. What is more, the man who claimed to be Andy Kaufman always went to great lengths to dissociate himself from the man who claimed to be Tony Clifton. In a *Los Angeles Times* article cited by Bill Zehme, Kaufman insisted that he was not Clifton and that he and Clifton were "two distinct personalities" (2001, 236). These rhetorical efforts to separate himself from his character are nicely illustrated by a minor episode that occurred on September 19, 1979, when Kaufman "sent" Clifton for a guest appearance on Dinah Shore's television show *Dinah!* As Bob Zmuda recalls, the guest stars on this afternoon variety show were usually "has-beens and B-grade performers on their way down and out," and since Kaufman had turned into a hipster icon by that time, the producers were supposedly "giddy that someone as hot as Andy Kaufman would deign to do their show in any guise" (Zmuda and Hansen 2001, 167). Considering the said "agenda" of the show, Kaufman's C-grade entertainer Tony Clifton was clearly more appropriate than any other character from his repertoire.

According to Zehme, what happened on *Dinah!* was not exactly dramatic. Tony Clifton was supposed to demonstrate how he would fry his favorite bacon and eggs in the studio, and while doing so, he simply handed the cracked eggshells over to the dumbfounded host.[9] Two days after this minor incident, Kaufman offered his apologies to Dinah Shore. However, he did not excuse himself for anything he did, but for the rude attitude of his colleague, insisting that since he was not Tony Clifton, he had absolutely nothing to do with the incident: "Tony Clifton is Tony Clifton and I am me" (Zehme 2001, 270). The problem with this is not that Kaufman's declaration about his identities is caught up in the rhetorical deadlock of tautology, with every signifier referring to nothing but itself. The real trouble is that even though Clifton's outward appearance makes him clearly recognizable as a travesty of the failed entertainer, he still raises questions of authenticity. Why is that?

The crucial point to note about Tony Clifton is the fact that the exact "biographical" origin of this character always remained obscure in terms of its fictional status. As Philip Auslander points out, Kaufman would claim "that Clifton was a real singer that he had initially impersonated as part of his own act but then hired as his opening act when he could afford to do so" (1992, 144). Kaufman often stated that he had discovered Tony Clifton on some stage in Las Vegas, and that his subsequent appearances in Clifton's guise were just his poor imitations of that original singer. Even if "Tony Clifton" had been a real biography of an unknown crooner, which was then appropriated by Kaufman, there would still be the trouble that the unknown original can hardly be told from his famous imitator.[10]

In the same year as the *Dinah!* incident reported above, the confusion surrounding Tony Clifton reached its climax at the end of Andy Kaufman's show at Carnegie Hall. Back on stage for an encore, Kaufman tells the audience that the Clifton whom they saw singing the "Star-Spangled Banner" as his opening act had in fact been the real Tony Clifton. Explaining to the audience that he discovered Clifton in Las Vegas in 1969 and that he "used to imitate him," Kaufman announces his original impersonation of Tony Clifton. He asks for a moustache, and otherwise unmasked, he starts to sing a song in Clifton's mumbling accent. Halfway into the song, Kaufman welcomes the "real" Clifton on the stage, at which point he is joined by that excessively made-up Tony Clifton who was previously seen performing the opening act.

Spectators at Carnegie Hall might have come up with two possible explanations for this doubling of Tony Clifton. In the naive version, they may have taken this second singer for that supposedly real Las Vegas singer on whose model Kaufman would claim to have built his parody called Tony Clifton. Otherwise, they might have guessed that it was Kaufman's collaborator Bob Zmuda or some other stage companion of his playing Tony Clifton in Kaufman's place. In retrospect, we know as a matter of course that the latter explanation is correct, but what really matters here is not the question of who this other Clifton was. Rather, the crucial question to ask at this point is how this act affected the relation between the Tony Clifton persona and Andy Kaufman, who was supposed to be the performer behind Clifton's makeup.

The moment when Clifton joins Kaufman on stage at Carnegie Hall, the supposed character is physically separated from its supposed author. Previously, the general assumption was that Andy Kaufman was present in disguise whenever Tony Clifton was performing. From now on, this was no longer a safe assumption, which meant that for Kaufman, there were even more ways of escaping as a performer. Opening up a space that separates the fictional persona from the allegedly real person on whom the former is said to be based, Kaufman vanished in the gap in between—and maybe this gap is even a nonspace of zero dimensions, because person and persona are in fact one and the same.

In light of episodes like this, Philip Auslander refers to the Tony Clifton character as a "media-produced simulacrum" (1992, 144). Indeed, is it not a perfect illustration of the simulacrum when Kaufman, at the end of his Carnegie Hall show, introduces the "real" Tony Clifton from Las Vegas, as opposed to what he claims is his own weak imitation (simulation) of that lounge singer? It is not possible to tell the fictional recreation of Tony Clifton from the real person it is supposedly based on, and so the very notions of copy and model are called into question in this simulacral performance of a character who is permanently suspended on the borderline between fiction and reality. Thus, Carnegie Hall marked that point in Kaufman's career when his Tony Clifton persona, by means of its own doubling, became more real and at the same time, paradoxically, more artificial.

However, the trouble caused by Tony Clifton was not only due to the fact that this figure seemed to be neither a real person nor a purely fictional character, and therefore, curiously, both real and fictional. Apart from this purely representational ambiguity, there was also the obscene excess displayed by Tony Clifton's sheer physical presence. The year before his Carnegie Hall show, Kaufman started working on *Taxi* on the condition that Clifton would be hired as a guest actor for at least two episodes that did not feature Kaufman's Latka; the singer did show up on the set, but prior to shooting the tenth episode, he was fired due to unprofessional conduct.

As Tony Clifton was literally dragged off the set of *Taxi*, most accounts of this incident curiously focus on the troublesome "realness" of his physical presence. When Judd Hirsch, a fellow actor on *Taxi*, recalls this incident, his statement suggests that the real trouble with Clifton was not that his presence was uncomfortable because his body was so obscene in a way reminiscent of Shakespeare's Falstaff character.[11] Hirsch notes that "the true body I was shoving off the stage was Andy Kaufman. Then I started to realize that I wasn't throwing out Andy Kaufman; I was throwing out Tony Clifton, which was a phantom, a fiction—a fiction with a real body" (Zehme 2001, 230).[12] So the real trouble was that the simulacral character that was Tony Clifton insisted on his own physical presence. What this incident illustrates, then, is that with Andy Kaufman, the performer could strictly not be "exorcised" from his personae. If his real body was possessed with the fictional "evil spirit" that was Tony Clifton, the real body had to be shoved off the stage in order to get rid of the disturbing fiction.

Kaufman's game of real-bodied fictions culminated in a twisted scene of doublings that did not feature Tony Clifton, but two physically near-identical Andys—one in the cute persona of Foreign Man, the other as the endearing host of a television show who reveals his rude "real self" as soon as he believes himself to be off the air. This episode occurs after the final scenes from *The Andy Kaufman Show* (1983), Kaufman's contribution to the PBS concert series *Soundstage*, which Zehme appreciates as the "most elliptical and surreal refraction of existential realities" that Kaufman ever created (2001, 340). While the final credits are still rolling, the host played by Kaufman, while gently waving goodbye and keeping his nice smile, starts to insult his viewers in front of their television sets. Mocking his home audience for their stupidity and ignorance, he calls them "idiots" and a "bunch of sheep" that would do whatever they are told. Once the final credits are over and the host is done with his verbal insults, he goes backstage, where, thinking he is off the air, he starts to harass his crew. At this point, Foreign Man joins the host, and in front of the backstage camera, he confronts him about his bad, unfriendly attitude. Thus, thanks to a simple filming technique that enables "plain" Andy Kaufman and Kaufman-as-Foreign-Man to literally face each other, an actual dispute ensues between the two. At the time *The Andy Kaufman Show* was produced, Foreign Man had long been transformed into Latka for *Taxi*, which is why this persona was commonly understood to be one of Kaufman's fictional characters by the time this special was aired on July 15, 1983.

At first, it is nice Foreign Man versus rude Andy, and the former politely reproaches the latter for his rude behavior, arguing that not only does he risk ruining his own career, but he also ruins the chances for Foreign Man to be loved by the public. Expressing his concern that Andy is in fact a "shy little man" with a "gentle soul" who wears his "tough-guy façade" only to hide his "insecurity," Foreign Man wants to persuade Andy to drop this boorish mask: "When you come to terms with your own deficiencies," he tells him, "then you'll be able to accept your true self and you won't have to hide behind this macho act." Upon this, tough Andy Kaufman finally collapses in front of his own fictional creation, bursting into tears, and when he walks out of the picture sobbing, cute Foreign Man is left alone to say goodbye to the home audience. In his exceedingly nice demeanor, he sweetly purrs, "Be good," waves his hand, and even blows a kiss.

This is not the end of the scene, though. As soon as Foreign Man is finished with his formal courtesies, he asks whether he is "off the air," and this is where Foreign Man, for his part, suddenly reveals a different persona, acting like a thug and asking his crew members for a wrestling match. Thus, the "tough-guy façade" that was Andy's mask has switched onto the face of Foreign Man, who is finally unmasked to be still "other" than we have presumed him to be. Ultimately, what this scene shows is that not even those personae that one has come to think of as completely fictional are reliable enough in the sense of representations of a coherent

"When you come to terms with your own deficiencies, then you'll be able to accept your true self." Foreign Man (*right*) confronts Andy Kaufman (*left*) about his "tough-guy façade" at the end of *The Andy Kaufman Show* (Rhino Home Video, 1983).

subject. Andy Kaufman's permanent displacement of identities even "infects," or "haunts" his supposedly consistent fictional characters. Hence, Michael Nash may have a point arguing that Kaufman portrayed "television as a hall of mirrors, an infinitization of itself" (1990, 10), though he stops short of the more radical implication of Kaufman's performance. Ultimately, it was the notion of personal identity that Kaufman portrayed as a "hall of mirrors," and the result of this was that he produced himself as an "infinitization of *him*self," not of television.

But then again, there he suddenly was—the real Andy. Six years before *The Andy Kaufman Show*, in the year preceding the Tony Clifton incident on the set of *Taxi*, Kaufman was commissioned to produce a television show entitled *The Midnight Special*

"Andy Kaufman is me. I'm Andy Kaufman." The "real" Andy on the couch in *The Midnight Special* (Sony Music Entertainment, 1981).

(1981) for NBC. Right at the beginning of this show, Kaufman is casually sitting on a sofa, totally unmasked, it seems, wearing everyday clothes and no makeup. In contrast with the public performance context of the rest of the special, the setting of this opening scene is markedly private, and here on the sofa it seems that the performer explicitly identifies himself as who he is, though Kaufman does so in the mode of his curiously anti-Rimbaudian tautological proposition: "Andy Kaufman is me. I'm Andy Kaufman."

Yet again, there is something suspicious about the tautological structure of this reference to a pure and undisguised subject that is in no way "other" than himself. After all, this footage showing "pure" Andy is intercut several times into the actual show, and things get more intricate when the special features Andy wrestling women on stage.[13] As a wrestler, Andy explicitly states that this part of the show is not a "comedy routine," insisting that "this is not a skit, this is real." But then again, these wrestling scenes on stage are followed by footage of the "real" Andy on the sofa, offering his comments on his performances as a wrestler. This is where the wrestler who insists on the realness of his act is unmasked by this "unmasked" Andy who, for his part, insists that his supposedly "real" wrestling stunt was all about not breaking character and that he was just playing the villain all along. This confession culminates in what came to be known as Andy Kaufman's "fundamentalist" credo as a performer: "I'm not breaking character, I'm not giving away to the audience that I'm playing a role. I believe in playing it straight to the hilt."

However, the deferral of the performer's identities does not stop here. In the next scene with casual, unmasked Andy on the couch, the person whom the viewer believes to have recognized as the performer behind the wrestler and all his other stage representations is again revealed to be yet another character when he briefly offers some biographical detail about himself: "I was born on January 17, 1937," supposedly undisguised Andy proclaims on the sofa, inventing a slightly different personal history for himself. For while it is true that Kaufman's actual birthday was January 17, in fact he was born twelve years after the man sitting on the sofa who appears to be the real Andy.

Minute as this displacement may seem, it is still significant, as it shows in detail just how consistently Kaufman worked on his series of displaced identities. Just when it appears that the performer behind all the masks of identity that Kaufman puts on in the show is revealed, it proves to be yet another illusory kernel, and just when it appears that the chain of personae reaches its closure, the process of displaced identities is actually not at all halted. Incidentally, this dubiously "plain" Andy on the sofa is also the man who expresses what was often (mis)taken as Kaufman's confession about the true agenda of his performance work: "I've never told a joke in my life." Rest assured that he is lying?

At this point, a brief digression into the representational logic of stand-up comedy should prove fruitful. In stand-up, the relationship between the performer's self and the characters he represents on stage has always been recognized as particularly precarious. As John Limon points out, stand-up "comedians are not allowed to be either natural or artificial" (2000, 6). In other words, the codes of the genre require that the question whether a comedian is acting "in character" or whether he is posing as "himself" must remain suspended at all times in stand-up comedy. To a considerable extent, then, stand-up is based on a conflation of the categories of performer and his characters, and in this regard, Andy Kaufman's persistent efforts to blur the boundaries between himself and his personae appear to be very much in line with the conventional codes of stand-up comedy.

In his book *Comic Visions*, David Marc seems to contradict

Limon's point, arguing that stand-up relies on a massive investiture of the performer's self. Most notably, he claims that a "stand-up comedian addresses an audience as a naked self" (1989, 13). While the very notion of a "naked self" may have long been discarded as a myth, this point offers some useful theoretical implications when Marc refines his argument by saying that for a stand-up comic, "the self is text to a much greater degree than in representational drama" (18). At this point, Marc joins Limon's line of argument, because the notion of self as textual material implies the idea that whatever one might consider to be the "self" is in fact never naked, but always already constituted by discursive practices. Thus, he takes into account the vagaries between what Limon calls the "natural" and the "artificial."

If stand-up according to David Marc is a comic show that heavily draws on the performer's self, this means it is also inherently tautological in its structure: "Steve Martin is Steve Martin is Steve Martin" (13). If the comedian's self serves as the textual material that he works into his acts, then Andy Kaufman performed his "personal text" in the form of a *palimpsest*, writing his numerous selves all over himself to the extent that they blurred every conception of what might have been the "original" text of his self. In other words, even if "Steve Martin is Steve Martin is Steve Martin," this does not mean that we know who Steve Martin is, precisely because stand-up is all about this conflation of the difference between a performer and his characters. Yet with Kaufman, this suspension of difference is more complex (and consequently, more fascinating), because Andy Kaufman is not only Andy Kaufman—he is also Foreign Man is also Tony Clifton is not Tony Clifton is not Andy Kaufman is also a professional wrestler and so on.

Incidentally, Marc also parallels the "self-centered" performative stance of stand-up comedy with the representational logic of professional wrestling. Unwittingly invoking Kaufman, who started out in stand-up and turned himself into a wrestler later on in his career (see chapter 4), Marc argues that both genres are characterized by the fact that "the mask can't be pried loose from the face of the performer" (17). In this perspective, Andy Kaufman, usually considered some kind of "avant-garde" entertainer, suddenly seems like a comic who does not go against the conventional imperatives of the form of stand-up comedy, but strictly complies with these imperatives—which is precisely my point about Kaufman being an overconformist author. Whether in the context of comedy or in wrestling, he acted as a performer who ultimately did nothing but fulfill the doctrine of the respective form. Always letting his "masks" merge with the performer's "face," Kaufman was consistently "natural" and "artificial" at the same time, and in this sense, his acts were strictly, that is excessively, orthodox to such a degree that deeply troubled the respective "ideologies" of representations that inform stand-up comedy and wrestling.

Kaufman's displacement was simple, but crucial. As he applied not one but multiple masks that would merge with the face of his own self, he rendered visible the inconsistency inherent in these forms of performance. If the implicit code of both stand-up and wrestling requires that the mask cannot be pried loose from the performer's face, this results in a logic of self-identity, which should be no cause for trouble. But if a comic (or a wrestler, for that matter) displays a multiplicity of masks, this necessarily entails that a multiplicity of faces (of the performer's self) are produced in the process.

This is also where those contemporaneous critics who kept speculating about Kaufman's alleged schizophrenia totally miss the point. Clearly, the array of personae that Kaufman incorporated with a near-pathological refusal "to let the mask slip" is not a secondary effect, or a symptom produced by some supposed primary psychic disorder on the performer's part. If the representational code of stand-up is taken more seriously than it is prepared to be taken, it becomes evident that Kaufman's "schizophrenia" is in fact an effect of the conventions of stand-up. It is true that Kaufman adopted numerous masks of identity, but since the conventional code of the genre required the conflation of the mask and the self's face, the simple consequence was that every mask that Kaufman created for himself was also a new face, adding up to a multiplicity of selves. Hence, Kaufman's alleged "schizophrenic" tendency is in fact a secondary symptom of his primary overconformism with respect to the formal imperatives of comedy and wrestling.[14]

As an entertainer who relentlessly submersed himself into his various personae, Kaufman certainly enacted an unprecedented dissolution between performer and his characters, as Michael Nash has noted (1990, 6). But as a consequence of what Nash calls Kaufman's "play of undecidability" (2), his performance work also radically dispersed every idea that there might be any one positively identifiable subject among all of these self-representations. Still, it would not be accurate to say that Kaufman, unlike any other figure in popular entertainment, embodies the near-proverbial decentered subject of postmodernism. Rather, Kaufman is excessively "centered" at all times, as he is always very much "in the middle" of his personae. As a performer, he eludes us precisely in the space that stretches between the various self-representations that are his characters.

With Kaufman, the subjective substance of the performer cannot be told from the material of his acts, and by implication, it is impossible to situate any master-subject that is "in charge" of all the performances. When Bill Zehme writes that Kaufman's "real him, of course, was not the real real him, except in voice and eye movement" (2001, 193), this reminds one of Gilles Deleuze's theory of "intelligent materialism"—and in some kind of a Deleuzean aside, one could argue that Kaufman's performance work shows that the subject has no metaphysical "place," as his subjectivity resides in nothing but the physical "matter that bodies" him.[15]

On the other hand, Zehme betrays a certain nostalgia for the lost notion of self-identity when he speculates that "the real real [Andy Kaufman] was the existential puppeteer who decided what would happen whenever people were looking" (193). Apart from the fact that Zehme grants Kaufman an excessive amount of agency if he views him as a master manipulating his audience like puppets, the crucial point is that as a performer, Kaufman remains a blank precisely because that "existential puppeteer" never manifests himself. The vacancy that is his self persists, because the master-subject called Kaufman never actually materializes to fill the space between his self-representations. Vanishing among his own masks that are his faces, Andy Kaufman presents himself truly as a performer of hysteria.[16]

"There's other real mes":
Andy Kaufman's Theatre of Hysteria

Ever since the very first case studies on hysterics were published, one aspect that has always been noted is the strong alliance that links hysteria to theatricality. In her book *The Knotted Subject*, Elisabeth Bronfen cites one of Jean-Martin Charcot's students who pointed out that the hysteric is to be considered "an actress on stage, a *comedian*" (1998, 226, my italics). If the quasi-altered self-representations of the hysterical subject always involve a theatrical manifestation of sorts, it is the other way round for Andy Kaufman—his comedy, or performance art (or whatever you prefer to call it) is essentially a theatre of hysteria. As Bronfen remarks, the hysteric is a subject who disturbs the clear binary opposition that separates truth from simulation, as she "offers representations of the self that she is convinced are absolutely true at any given moment" (226). This finds its exact correlative in Andy Kaufman's notorious refusal to "break character." A truly hysterical performer, Kaufman acts according to his firm belief in the absolute, irreducible truth of his various personae.

If the seminal function of hysteria is basically to stage the doubt that the real self and the representations of that self may not be concurrent, Kaufman's performance work dissipates the very notion of any "real" self as well. As Bronfen points out further, "the hysteric produces a versatile and seemingly infinite array of self-representations," and through manipulation of these masks of the self, she "awakes the sense of how impossible it is to determine whether there is a consistent subject behind them" (39). This description of hysteria reads like a concise paraphrase of what is at stake in Kaufman's performance art. At any rate, it recalls the way the executive board at ABC reacted to *Andy's Funhouse*, which troubled them precisely because this lack of concurrence between the performer and his self-representations made it impossible to determine any "consistent subject" among Kaufman's masks.

However, in the context of a discussion of Andy Kaufman's performance art in terms of an enactment of hysterical gestures, it is not accurate any more to say that Kaufman simply "vanishes" among his various personae. Drawing on a definition offered by Stavros Mentzos, Bronfen points out that, ultimately, hysteria not only makes visible a "noncoincidence" between these quasi-altered selves and any real self, but in a more radical sense, the hysteric displays this noncoincidence to such an extent "that she not only plays roles but also her existence resides in the performance of these roles" (298). In hysteria, then, the very activity of enacting quasi-altered self-representations becomes the condition that defines the subject's existence.

In the year following the production of *Andy's Funhouse*, Kaufman explicitly discussed this issue as a guest on the *Tonight Show* on February 20, 1978. Having finished his act, Kaufman is interviewed by host Steve Martin, who asks him about the origin and the status of his various characters, starting some sort of meta-discourse about the logic of his theatre of hysteria:

ANDY KAUFMAN: What, which [character]?

STEVE MARTIN: The one out there that you did.

AK: Oh, no—that's really me.

SM: Ahhh. And then—

AK: The Foreign Man, you mean? That's another character.

SM: Mmmm-hmmm. So that was really you out there. And then what are you doing right now?

AK: Right now? This is really me.

SM: Oh. [*Audience laughter*] And then—now, what about the Foreign Man?

AK: No, that's not—that's just a character I do.

SM: Oh, I see. [*Laughter*] So there's two real yous, and then there's a character.

AK: Well, there's some others also—there's other real mes—but Foreign Man isn't one of 'em. (Zehme 2001, 198)

In some sense, this brief conversation prefigures yet another American version of the vacant subject of postmodernism, namely, the protagonist from the film *Zelig* (1983), Woody Allen's mock-biopic about a "human chameleon" who completely merges into his various environments, imitating the cultural codes of whoever happens to be around. In the film, Leonard Zelig is described as "a cipher, a nonperson, a performing freak," all of which basically reads like a shorthand version of how Andy Kaufman was viewed by his contemporaries. Although he is clearly no human chameleon in the sense of Zelig, Kaufman performs his various self-fashionings in a way that is strikingly analogous to Leonard Zelig's play of identities.

In *The Knotted Subject* Bronfen offers an intriguing analysis of *Zelig* that reveals striking analogies to Kaufman. Using the protagonist of the film as the model case for what Bronfen calls the "happy hysteric," she notes that Leonard Zelig belongs to an order of representations "that are pure simulacrums having nothing as their point of reference" (1998, 98, 43). Woody Allen's film, she argues, performs "an infinite mirroring of quasi-altered, self-representations" (49). As the dialogue above illustrates, the very same can be argued for Andy Kaufman, whose infinitization of himself could not be fixed at any "final referent" either. In fact, Bronfen's argument about Zelig proves perfectly compatible with the way Kaufman, by mirroring his simulacral self-representations, called into question the very notion of an original "self." If *Zelig* raises the question whether there is any such thing as a "true self," or whether the self ultimately amounts to nothing more than the constant *performance* of self-representations, then the film revolves around the same issues that are at stake in Kaufman's work as an entertainer—the crucial point being that both Kaufman and Allen's film refuse to provide an answer to this question, leaving their audience in a state of disturbing uncertainty about it.

What this suggests is that Leonard Zelig performs an over-conformist version of Lifton's "protean self." Incidentally, when Bronfen comments on Zelig's excessive proteanism, this reads like an analysis of Kaufman's conversation with Steve Martin on *The Tonight Show:* "By performing more than one quasi-altered self, [Zelig] actually dismantles the previous self-representation, and with it puts in question those he was imitating as well" (45).

This is just as pertinent in Kaufman's case, and in a way, Bronfen's point here is echoed in the opening scene from *Man on the Moon*. At the very beginning of the film, Jim Carrey as Foreign Man is standing in a blank studio set and urgently begging his audience to leave. Curiously introducing himself as "Andy," Foreign Man explains that the movie that was supposed to follow is terribly dumb, and in his charming stammer, he points out that "all of the most important things in my life are changed around and mixed up for dramatic purposes." Foreign Man then reveals that he "cut out all the baloney," which is why the movie is "much shorter" now—in fact, Foreign Man finally admits, "this is the end of the movie." Accordingly, the final credits start to roll onscreen, while Foreign Man plays a song on a gramophone. Eventually, he slams it shut, at which point the screen goes completely black.

A period of dead air ensues, which lasts for about fifteen seconds. After this stretch of silence, Jim Carrey peeks in from the left. Apparently playing "normal" Andy Kaufman now, he takes the "stage" again, telling the audience (with no foreign accent this time) that the previous scene was merely an act to get rid of those people in the audience "who just wouldn't understand me—and don't even want to try." In his crucial line, he then cheerfully remarks that the movie is actually not terrible at all, but "filled with colorful characters—like the one I just did, and the one I'm doing now." Anticipating the permanent deferral of positively identifiable selves that the protagonist will perform during the entire film, this opening scene from *Man on the Moon* exposes both the previous and the current quasi-altered self-representations as "not real," and thus offers a condensed version of what is also at stake in *Zelig*.[17]

Expanding this parallel reading of Kaufman and Zelig a little further, I would like to invoke what Bronfen calls the pictorial "navel" of Allen's film. Referring to the only two portraits that exist of Leonard Zelig, she argues that these photographs "actually enact the subject escaping" (1998, 46). While this would serve perfectly well as a catchphrase for Andy Kaufman's work as a "postmodern escape artist," the difference is that in *Zelig* the trajectory of the narrative runs toward that moment of catharsis when the vacant, chameleon-like subject who has no positive self-content is finally cured of this "disorder." For Zelig, the cure for what is literally his "self-defect" is ultimately a matter of discarding his previous strategy of adaptation. Recovering from his obsessive compulsion to merge with his cultural environment, he eventually learns to act according to an individualism that is more properly "American." In the end, Bronfen points out, Zelig "has learned to imitate the dominant cultural ideology that privileges the role of the individualist who speaks up and says what is on his mind, whereas earlier he had acted the chameleon who blends in" (51). Having overcome his compulsion to identify with whatever that surrounds him, Zelig has experienced a successful conversion to America's predominant ideological discourse of self-making.

However, is not this conversion ultimately just another act of adaptation in a culture that favors the self-made individualist over the "human chameleon"? This is precisely Bronfen's point when she argues that while *Zelig* dismantles the "fantasy that a subject can be his own man" as what she calls a "precarious protective fiction" (51), Allen's film also sustains this very fantasy. In the excessively protean simulations and dissimulations of their performances, "happy hysterics" like Leonard Zelig obliquely articulate the traumatic knowledge that they successfully evade, embracing the protective fiction that the subject can always re-create himself.

Implicitly, this brings me to the "political" dimension of hysteria, that is, the question of how the hysteric may effectively function as a critic who subverts dominant ideological discourses.

In his *Dictionary of Lacanian Psychoanalysis*, Dylan Evans defines the hysterical subject as "precisely someone who appropriates another's desire by identifying with them" (2001, 79). With regard to the potential of subversion implied in this structure of desire, Slavoj Žižek points out that Jacques Lacan, in accordance with Freud's position, always insisted that hysteria poses much more serious threats to predominant public discourses than the attitude of perversion (1999, 247). Unlike the pervert, whose desire to openly stage the "dark" fantasies only serves to sustain these discourses, the hysteric succeeds in disrupting the implicit ideology of any given culture because she "articulates the gnawing doubt whether secret desires really contain what they promise" (248). Appropriating another's desire, the hysterical subject functions like a screen that mirrors this desire in such a way as to question if it truly holds what it promises.

Hence, the symptoms displayed by the hysteric are always an imitation of those cultural discourses that produced these symptoms in the first place. This is why Bronfen suggests that hysteria must not only be regarded in the classic sense of a "malady of representation," but more specifically, has to be understood as an "illness of mimesis" (1998, 40, 44). Andy Kaufman is precisely such a hysterical imitator who functions strictly mimetically with respect to the predominant public discourse that is the American Dream. Absolutely identifying with the mode of subjectivity proposed by this communal fantasy, Kaufman appropriates, and thus questions, the desire prescribed by the American Dream.

But first, this argument should be rephrased more specifically for the context of stand-up comedy. As Kaufman's Foreign Man used to parody the standard routine of "imitating" celebrities or politicians, he would also take too literally the representational logic of stand-up. In *The Andy Kaufman Special* (1977), for instance, Foreign Man "imitates" Archie Bunker and Ed Sullivan, and later in *The Midnight Special* (1981), he delivers his "impressions" of Ronald Reagan and Steve Martin. Of course, though, charmingly inept Foreign Man impersonates each of these celebrities without dropping his exotic accent, which means that he does not actually mimic his objects of ridicule, but what he imitates are the very gestures of imitation, that is, he mimics the routine of stand-up "impressions." In these parodies of parodies, Foreign Man truly stages a "malady of mimesis," as his impersonations do not work as mocking imitations of their points of reference, but they practically stage their very failure in terms of the mimetic code of stand-up "impressions." In other words, Foreign Man does not imitate the celebrities themselves, but he mimics (and therefore, hysterically questions) the very discourse of stand-up comedy and the extent to which it relies on imitations for enjoyment.[18]

Unlike the poor mimicry performed by Foreign Man, who questions the code of stand-up comedy by not meeting the standards of conventional impressions, Kaufman's enactment of the American Dream of self-invention is totally accurate. In the sense that he actually mirrors the predominant public discourse, Kaufman brings to light its inherent inconsistencies in a mode of subversion that clearly functions according to the logic of hysteria. In Bronfen's words, the subversive thrust of the hysterical performer consists in the fact that "the inconsistent number of masks she dons actually displays the inconsistency of the symbolic system ruled by the paternal metaphor" (1998, 39). In an effort to translate this into the ideological discourse of the American Dream, I argue that the predominant cultural "metaphor" that informs America's public discourses is the "makeover" of the self, that is, the notion that the subject has the opportunity to endlessly re-create himself. Kaufman performed this ideological imperative of his culture (the American Dream) up to its too-literal extreme, and in effect, its seemingly "healthy" promise of finding happiness by way of a "protean" self-enactment took the form of a disease—pushed to its turning point, the offer of permanent self-invention shows its uncanny flipside, namely, an unstoppable, virus-like proliferation of American identities.

In *The Protean Self* Lifton briefly elaborates on this kind of "extremist" proteanism, which he dismisses as the "negative" or "caricatured" proteanism of a fragmented self. In Lifton's words, fragmentation as a caricature of proteanism entails a radical loss of "coherence and continuity, an extreme expression of dissociation" (1993, 202). According to Lifton, the production of multiple personalities may then function as a protective shield against the threat of total disintegration inflicted on the self by such fragmentation, and as one possible effect of this pathological, "sick" form of proteanism, this "fragmented self is neither centered nor decentered, but *uncentered*" (206, italics in original). As far as Andy Kaufman's performance work is concerned, Lifton would probably argue that far from enacting a "healthy" form of American proteanism, Kaufman stages a protean self that has fallen victim to its own fragmentation—ultimately, an exemplary caricature of proteanism.

What is particularly significant about these passages is the way Lifton relates multiple personality to proteanism "gone awry." As regards the phenomenon of multiple personality, he argues that this clinical structure designates the psychic stage where "the protean process has been *literalized* to the point of caricature" (209, my italics). This form of "literalism," Lifton points out, is one of the essential elements of fundamentalism, because the fundamentalist subject is someone who lives in strict accordance with a "literalized doctrine" (10). In precisely this sense, Andy Kaufman emerges as the fundamentalist American Dreamer who takes the ideological doctrine of this communal fantasy by its word. By excessively conforming to its imperative to refashion oneself in a potentially endless procedure of "proteanism," Kaufman takes the American Dream to the extreme of literalism—and this overorthodoxy is what makes him a subversive hysteric, as he stages the threat of dissociation that is washed over in the seemingly "happy" version of the explicit ideological text.

Finally, then, what Andy Kaufman displays is how America's ideological imperative to produce endless reinventions of oneself works according to the logic of a double bind. The manifest aspect of this logic is that part of the Dream that says that in America we are free to re-create ourselves, and that this is the way to succeed on our pursuit of happiness—but what is occluded is the fact that our self is bound to multiply and dissolve in the process of these self-inventions. If Kaufman ends up as a caricature of American proteanism, this is just a necessary effect of his most faithful enactment of the promise of self-invention as represented in the American Dream. In the final instance, this promise produces *serial subjects* that are effectively evacuated in their own self-representations. This is how Kaufman renders visible one of the fundamental inconsistencies of the American Dream, and in the sense of the evacuation that this seriality implies, he is indeed structurally analogous to the vacant self of "serial killer" Patrick Bateman from *American Psycho*.[19]

Along with this, Kaufman offers a new perspective on one of the most prominent stock figures of American popular culture, namely, the hero who suffers from a doubling of his self.[20] In the light of Kaufman's performance work, the trouble that this kind of a doubled self entails seems like a relatively "safe" version of the American Dream of self-invention, because the double remains suspended in a binary opposition and therefore still supports the idea of an imaginary center of the subject. On the other hand, Kaufman's disturbingly consistent displacement of identities shows that the truly unsettling thing is the multiplicity of selves that necessarily follows if one were to take the doctrine of the American Dream by its word and turn oneself into a serial subject.[21]

The Believer as Victim and "That Other Andy"

As a conclusion for this chapter about Kaufman and the mode of serial subjectivity, two postscripts: If Kaufman took the American injunction to "live the Dream" by its word, and thus became the performer of a version of the American Dream that was too literal (and thus, too familiar) for the public to bear, then paradoxically, the opposite is also true. It may be the case that Kaufman enacted too literally the fantasy of permanent self-invention as represented by the American Dream, but at the same time, his performance art was also not literal enough for himself to survive in the commercial context of comedy. After all, his commercial failure as a comedian was not only due to his refusal to be a "proper" comic at all, nor was it because of his refusal to give any sense of coherent self, rendering any consistent identification on the part of the audience totally impossible. Arguably, Kaufman failed to fulfill the commercial requirements of the comedy circuit because he did not produce ever-new *material* as a comic performer.

Two quotes from reviews of Kaufman's show at Carnegie Hall may serve to illustrate this point. In the *Los Angeles Times*, a journalist argued that Kaufman quite simply "is going to have to come up with fresher material" (Zehme 2001, 243). Regarding the same show, the *Variety* reviewer pointed out that Kaufman "creates a series of characters which depend, at least in part, on audience unfamiliarity with Kaufman as Kaufman to succeed." Arguing that the effectiveness of Kaufman's Tony Clifton acts is undermined by media coverage, this critic claims that it is "time for Kaufman to come up with a new Clifton" (242). After all, comedy not only wants routines and material, but it always wants new material that is recognizable as routine.

While Kaufman was able to produce a disturbing array of personae that dissimulated any sense of the performer's kernel of identity, his comic routines and material appeared to be limited to a degree that blocked commercial success within the context of comedy. It seems a little paradoxical, then, that the man who went too far in his production of different self-representations did not go far enough in creating new routines for himself. Toward the end of his career, before his cancer diagnosis, Kaufman joined a professional wrestling tour, and Bill Zehme's comments on this final chapter of Andy Kaufman's performing career speak for themselves: "Nobody paid much attention. He kept on screaming and strutting. He had disappeared. Nobody cared" (2001, 342). So it turns out that Kaufman's enactment of the fantasy of self-invention was both too literal and not literal enough, and finally, this may well be the truly tragic paradox of his career. Not only did he faithfully perform the free play of serial subjectivities as offered by the ideological narrative of the American Dream, but to some extent, he also turned out as its victim.

In this curious double bind, Kaufman's career recalls Renata Salecl's analysis of Andrei Chikatilo, notorious serial killer from the former Soviet Union. In her psychoanalytical reading of the Chikatilo murder case, Salecl draws attention to the killer's "desire to find clues for his acts in the Soviet system, in which he was always a true believer, even though, in his view, he was also its victim" (1994, 107). In a slightly modified form, Andy Kaufman represents precisely this figure of the "true believer" who regards himself as the victim of an ideological discourse. But contrary to Chikatilo, who considered himself a victim *despite* the fact that he firmly believed in the system, Kaufman has never been able to escape his destiny as a victim of the "system" (in this case, the

American Dream) precisely *because* he enacted its innermost collective fantasies in a way that any overorthodox believer would. As the fundamentalist "believer" who takes the ideological imperative of the American Dream by its word, Kaufman is also victimized by it, and necessarily so, because this Dream is a fantasmatic narrative and, therefore, ultimately impossible.

My second postscript involves a brief cross-mapping of Kaufman's obsessional deferral of identities with that other, more famous Andy, called Warhol. To some extent, Warhol bears an affinity to Kaufman as far as his public persona is concerned. Evacuating his own self in an effort to drain it of any positive content, Warhol also enacted a gesture that signals that at the core of his subjectivity, there may have been nothing but a traumatic void. As Hal Foster phrases it in *The Return of the Real*, "the fascination of Warhol is that one is never certain about this subject behind: is anybody home, inside the automaton?" (1996, 131). One could easily substitute "Kaufman" for "Warhol" here. Warhol and Kaufman both presented themselves as figures of "nonsubjectivity," so as far as the effect of his public image is concerned, the negation of positive subjectivity as performed by Warhol is strictly analogous to Kaufman's persistent deferral of whatever his "real" self might have been.

What is entirely different, though, is the process by which this effect of the nonsubject is produced. Andy Kaufman hysterically produces an array of signifiers of various identities, and then he sets these in motion in order to unmask the "original" subject as a phantom. With Kaufman, the subject is rendered as a fantasmatic category that we construct for ourselves in order to keep the traumatic knowledge of our constitutive void at bay. Warhol, on the other hand, works hard to empty himself out of any signifiers of identity precisely in order to turn his own persona into the ultimate signifier of that void. Thus, if he "posed as a blank screen," as Foster puts it (261n), Warhol turned himself into the perfect object of projected identifications. Instead of performing the permanent invention of selves the way Kaufman did, Warhol invited his "audience" to become the interpreters, or performers, of his own self. With Warhol, it is always the others who project possible identities onto him, the perfectly blank screen, the simulacrum, the ultimate phantom of what we call the subject.

In this sense of how they both enact their respective personae, Warhol and Kaufman can be said to represent two sides of one and the same coin—and in a way, Warhol's public persona presents itself as an inversion of how Kaufman enacts the dimension of self-invention as offered by the American Dream. While Kaufman's strategy is to keep inventing and performing his selves in his own right, Warhol invites others to invent and perform instead of himself, and this is reflected by the process of production that marks their respective works. Does not Kaufman's one-man show of serial subjects curiously appear like an inversion of the Factory, where Warhol dissolved any sense of his artistic identity by employing an entire staff to produce art objects for him? Kaufman, on the other hand, dissolved any sense of identity by employing an entire staff of personae. While Andy Warhol delegated his artistic activity to the external corporate body of the workers from his Factory, Kaufman employed his own body as his "factory," and the various subjects were the artistic objects that were serially produced this body/factory. Warhol represented the passive supervisor who employed his personal factory, whereas Kaufman actively ran the factory that was made up of his own personae.

At this point, the notion of *interpassivity* as proposed by Robert Pfaller is helpful. Coined in analogy to the more common idea of interactivity, the term *interpassivity* designates a peculiarly "negative" economy of enjoyment whereby we appoint someone or something to enjoy in our place, involving prosthetics of enjoyment, which Pfaller refers to as "machines of enjoyment" (2000, 2, my translation). A well-known example for this kind of transfer is the phenomenon of canned laughter used in television sitcoms; as the medium produces its own laughter, it effectively spares us the trouble to laugh ourselves, but curiously enough, what we enjoy about sitcoms is precisely the fact that their ready-made laughter liberates us from enjoyment. However, as Slavoj Žižek points out in his essay on interpassivity, the subject who delegates his enjoyment by means of an interpassive transfer is truly and radically decentered "because interpassivity deprives me of the innermost kernel of my substantial identity" (2000, 27, my translation). If it is no longer the subject who enjoys him- or herself, but some prosthetic device that enjoys *for* the subject, then this interpassive transfer amounts to a most fundamental evacuation of the self. In what way does this notion of interpassivity pertain to Kaufman and Warhol?

If Andy Kaufman's series of invented selves constitutes a literal enactment of the fantasmatic narratives promised by the American Dream, these same promises of multiple identities are also at stake with Andy Warhol, however *ex negativo*. In Warhol's case, these self-formations are not actively lived through by the subject, because this subject "is not there," except as an empty vessel. Instead, it is the others who actively fill his self with positive content by way of identifications projected onto his blank façade of nonsubjectivity. In other words, Andy Warhol "outsources" any enactment of subjectivity, and thanks to this process of transferred activity, he need not even bother about his own enjoyment, because it is the others who enjoy in his stead. If Warhol even drains himself of his enjoyment and thus represents the "interpassive performer" *par excellence*, Andy Kaufman both actively lives and enjoys according to the American imperative of self-invention.[22]

This ultimately brings me back to the inherent paradox of the American Dream. This communal fantasy offers the promise of constant reinvention of the self as a means to find enjoyment, but its inherent double bind consists in the fact that the true realization of this fantasy would require a frantic activity of self-invention that makes the very thing that the fantasy offers impossible. The fundamental paradox that haunts any true subject of the American Dream is that the injunction to enjoy one's serial selves actually evacuates one as a subject, and both Kaufman and Warhol serve as illustrations of this point. Though they are both "successful" in their compliance with the American Dream, the impossibility of its ideological promise materializes in the fact that they both have to pay a price. Warhol, who is nothing but a blank screen, ends up being no longer part of his own self, as it were. As for Kaufman, the final chapter of this book will show that even as he sticks to the continuous drill in self-making prescribed by the letter of the American Dream, he can do so only at the expense of repeatedly inducing his own symbolic death.

Finally, Andy Kaufman's mode of serial subjectivity also renders visible the implications of the fact that the American Dream is actually nothing more than an empty gesture. As Žižek points out in *The Plague of Fantasies*, every ideological discourse is based on an operation of symbolic exchange which relies on "a gesture made to be rejected" every once in a while (1997, 28). If America tells us that we can/must "live the Dream," it is our very rejection of this "empty" offer that makes this ideological imperative work in the first place. Conversely, if we take this empty gesture by its word and accept the offer to "live the Dream," as Kaufman did, this literal understanding of the symbolic exchange has the potential to truly shatter the ideological frame. According to Žižek, if the subject treats "the forced choice as a true choice," he effectively "suspends the phantasmic frame of unwritten rules which tell him how to choose freely" (29). The consequences of this suspension are invariably catastrophic, Žižek points out, and he suggests that the literal understanding of such an empty (symbolic) offer might be one way to reach what Lacan terms *la traversée du fantasme*.

However, a certain "subjective" precondition is necessary for this suspension to become operative in the first place. The traversal of the fantasy, Žižek writes, consists "in an acceptance of the fact that *there is no secret treasure in me*, that the support of me (the subject) is purely phantasmic" (10, italics in original). The subject as radical negativity, as constitutive void—this is what Andy Kaufman stages in the fundamentalist proteanism of his enactment of proverbial American identities, and their continuous proliferation. If there is no secret treasure in Kaufman, if there is no "Rosebud" to be excavated, as screenwriters Scott Alexander and Larry Karaszewski found out, this is ultimately because Andy Kaufman represents the most devoted subject of the American Dream that one can imagine.

CHAPTER 4

Celebrity Deathmatch

I'm a bigger nobody than I was before.

—Mark David Chapman

The Midnight Special (1981) features a brief sequence that shows Andy Kaufman working as a busboy at Jerry's Famous Deli. "I always like to set aside some time for being a busboy," Kaufman explains, to keep in touch with the ordinary people and to overcome the separation between performer and the public. If this is Andy's nonglamorous "other job," its purpose is to help him compensate for the proverbial loss of "hard" reality that every entertainer is said to suffer in the illusory world of show business.

No matter how factual or fictional these scenes are, this "biographical" detail from *The Midnight Special* marks the most explicit overlap of the two dimensions of Kaufman's excessively literal enactment of the American Dream. Apart from the fact that Kaufman's job as a busboy constitutes yet another episode in his series of self-representations, this secondary profession clearly quotes the most popular version of the trajectory of personal success that designates the imaginary objective of the American Dream. After all, what Kaufman stages here is the proverbial narrative of the rags-to-riches career, with its implications of fame and stardom—but strangely enough, he does so in a way that presents the two conditions of this trajectory as simultaneous. It is not that Kaufman retroactively invents a personal prehistory in the lower-class segment of society in order to make his subsequent rise to stardom seem more glamorous, but rather he presents himself as a successful show-business performer who, at the same time, also works as a busboy. This part-time busboy that is Kaufman is not an earlier incarnation of Kaufman the entertainer, but the two coexist at the same time, and by means of this synchronicity, this performance effectively undermines the sequential logic of the rags-to-riches myth.[1]

In terms of its ideological function, the proverbial myth of success is clearly one of the most powerful aspects of the American Dream. In his supplementary chapter in Richard Dyer's book *Stars*, Paul McDonald notes that the most important structural function of the rags-to-riches narrative is that it promises the possibility of stardom, but at the same time, it "obscures the conditions of exploitation" that sustain the star system (1998, 197). While it is certainly true that the ideological text of the myth of success conceals the conditions of exploitation, I would argue that the more fundamental operation enacted by this mythical narrative consists in its implicit denial of social differences. As Dyer points out in *Stars*, the rags-to-riches narrative is based on the belief that in America the class-system does not apply: "The general meaning of the myth of success is that American society is sufficiently open for anyone to get to the top, regardless of rank" (42). Based on the idea of a democracy of stardom, the rags-to-riches narrative purports that everybody can make his or her fortune and become a star, regardless of social status, and this is precisely what makes it such a powerful ideological apparatus in the sense of Louis Althusser. For this is where the American Dream is most explicitly a public discourse that represents the imaginary relationship of subjects to their real social conditions.

Kaufman, by literally enacting the American myth that

everyone has equal opportunities to become a star, articulates the inconsistencies that are obscured by its promise of success. As Philip Auslander has noted, Kaufman's performance art often deconstructs the cult of celebrity while at the same time exploiting it (1992, 150). By implication, the two biographical "curves" of the myth of success are always curiously intertwined in his work. With Kaufman, the issues of rise and fall, as well as success and failure, are often presented as strangely simultaneous. Even at the height of his celebrity, Kaufman's performances render visible the unacknowledged underpinnings of the star system, with its vast numbers of failures, "has-beens," and "not-yets" (the latter being invariably destined to end up as "never-will-bes").

At the beginning of this book, while referring to Foreign Man's inability to tell a joke, I have briefly discussed the notion of failure in the context of stand-up comedy. Later on, there was Tony Clifton, this obscene incarnation of the never-quite-risen star who embodies a disconcerting byproduct of the American myth of success, the "abject" of the star system. However, not all of Kaufman's acts that explicitly dealt with show-business failures are exercised by one of his own characters. In his television specials, as well as in his Carnegie Hall show, Kaufman employs some of his guests to reveal the miserable, nonglamorous flipside of the star system.

Early on in *Andy Kaufman Plays Carnegie Hall* (1979), Kaufman introduces an African American street singer on stage, offering him the proverbial "chance of a lifetime" to become a star. The man, he informs his audience, usually sings "Happy New Year" for passersby on Times Square, but now he is allowed to perform his song in front of a large audience of people who have actually paid money to see the show. As the host of his variety show, Kaufman introduces this special guest appearance as if it were an act of sheer generosity on his part, but in point of fact, his gesture comes across as cruel and exploitative. It may be true that Kaufman turns this unknown street entertainer into a "star" for a few minutes, granting him the opportunity to present his talents at Carnegie Hall, but at the same time, there is no doubt about the fact that this momentary glimpse of "stardom" will be so short-lived that in the end, Kaufman will have deprived his guest of what he cannot have anyway, namely, a successful career in show business. To put it more succinctly, it is precisely Kaufman's "generous" gesture that functions as the stumbling block for this street singer to truly become a star. Although the truth about this scene is only established retroactively, it is clear that at the very moment when the man could be "reborn" as a star in the entertainment business, he is already irretrievably falling into oblivion.

Andy Warhol, who was among the audience at Carnegie Hall, must have been delighted by the implications of this scene. Not only did Kaufman enact Warhol's now-proverbial aphorism that everyone will enjoy fifteen minutes of fame, but he also staged the sense of tragedy that haunts this dictum. At the same time that Kaufman bestows the blessings of celebrity on this street singer, he also fulfills the miserable consequences that are left unspoken in Warhol's prophecy. The first implication that is often disregarded about Warhol's aphorism concerns the disappearance of the audience: After all, who is still willing to watch if everybody is a star or wants to be one? However, what is at stake here is the second, more uncanny consequence, which concerns the fact that if everybody will be famous for fifteen minutes, then everybody will have to sink into oblivion immediately after. Hence, just as the promise of immortality signified by stardom is about to fulfill itself, the street singer is already dead for show business, and in retrospect, he is always already lost and buried in entertainment history.[2]

If oblivion is the unacknowledged flipside that sustains the star system, this becomes even more prevalent in another of

Kaufman's conceptual routines, namely, the segment called "Has-Been Corner" as featured in *The Andy Kaufman Special* (1977) and *The Andy Kaufman Show* (1983). In the former, Kaufman welcomes one Gail Slobodkin, a former child actress who supposedly made an uncredited appearance on a Broadway production of *The Sound of Music*. After her debut, Kaufman informs his audience, Mrs. Slobodkin's "career kind of fizzled into oblivion," and the following conversation between the host and his guest is not exactly an interview, but an unmerciful investigation into the conditions of oblivion: "What was it like when you first realized that you weren't going to make it in show business?" This is Kaufman's first question, and in an even more straightforward way, he then asks: "How does it feel to be a has-been?"

Eventually, the awkward conversation ends with Kaufman expressing his best wishes for Mrs. Slobodkin's future in the entertainment business: "I hope that you make it. I really do. Personally, I don't think you will." As this additional remark generates laughter from the studio audience, the woman is definitely branded as a show-business failure, but since the scene itself occurs in the context of entertainment, it shows more than just Kaufman's degradation of one of his guests. In a cheerfully irreverent way, this scene articulates the discontent inherent in the public discourse of stardom—a discourse that can only reproduce itself as a version of the American myth of success on the condition that its underpinnings embodied by failures and has-beens are obscured. Strictly speaking, Mrs. Slobodkin is not degraded by Andy Kaufman, but by her inability to live up to the ideological promise of the American Dream. Kaufman, for his part, simply acts as the mouthpiece of this Dream.

As another guest in the "Has-Been Corner," *The Andy Kaufman Show* features one Jim Brandy, whom Kaufman introduces as a singer who "was somewhat big in the late '50s," when he allegedly "made the top twenty all across the country" with a song called "Wild Wild Lovin'." Yet this moderate charts success is immediately undermined as the host points out that Brandy entered the charts at a time when Elvis Presley was doing military service in Germany, Kaufman's argument being that the void Elvis left in American pop music came to be filled with poor substitutes for the King. Adding that Jim Brandy was once voted "most promising singer of the year" and that he was generally expected to become a "big star," Kaufman welcomes his guest on stage, and when he asks him how he feels considering "all the success that you had and were supposedly going to have and you never had," Brandy awkwardly smiles and admits that it feels "lousy" and "not great." In short, the scene is embarrassing.

Jim Brandy in the "Has-Been-Corner," performing his supposed hit record "Wild Wild Lovin'." From *The Andy Kaufman Show* (Rhino Home Video, 1983).

But maybe the entire situation is just another of Kaufman's elaborate fictions. When the singer performs two songs at the end of his appearance in *The Andy Kaufman Show*, a number of clues apparently confirm this suspicion: Mr. Brandy's shaky intonation when he sings the ballad "The Nearness of You," and when he once again performs his supposed hit record, "Wild Wild Lovin'," he does not remember the lyrics, and he has to put on a pair of glasses in order to read the words from a piece of paper. Extensive research on Brandy's supposed hit single brings no result, so maybe the whole story about his mediocre charts success is indeed a fiction, and "Jim Brandy" is simply a more heartbreaking version of obnoxious Tony Clifton.

But then again, the former child actress introduced in *The Andy Kaufman Special* as "Gail Slobodkin" might as well be an actress hired to play a former child actress who failed to succeed as an adult. As any information about these "has-beens" can hardly be verified, one is left to wonder if they are real show-business failures or fake biographies scripted by Kaufman. There persists a fundamental uncertainty regarding the authenticity of the "failures" that are exposed in the "Has-Been Corner," and this is precisely what makes Kaufman's critique of celebrity culture so poignant in the first place. If the very concept of stardom is based on conditions of exploitation that need to be obscured for the star system to work, then nothing could articulate this more strongly than the ambiguity about the fictional or factual status of the biographies presented in the "Has-Been Corner."

With these performances, Kaufman not just offered a critique of America's ongoing obsession with celebrity culture, but in some sense, he also anticipated present-day television shows such as MTV's *Becoming* and the *Where Are They Now?* series on VH1. Celebrating yesterday's pop stars and offering information about their current activities, *Where Are They Now?* may seem like a less disrespectful version of what is at stake in Kaufman's "Has-Been Corner," but there is an important structural difference between the two formats. Clearly, there is a strong sense of nostalgia about the way *Where Are They Now?* deals with has-beens, but this is not what sets it apart from Kaufman's parody *avant la lettre*. The crucial aspect about *Where Are They Now?* is that the celebrities portrayed are always positively identifiable as who they are, namely, half-forgotten stars of yore. While their days of success may long be over, there is no doubt that at one time, these has-beens did have their share of stardom, because they are half-remembered, at least. In this respect, the portraits on *Where Are They Now?* are fundamentally different from the fundamental oblivion embodied by the guests in Kaufman's "Has-Been Corner," where the past success of a formerly promising "star" like Jim Brandy is always suspected to be a fiction in the first place. Presenting the specters of those who are truly forgotten, the "Has-Been Corner" is Kaufman's pre-emptive critique of the pacified versions of oblivion offered by *Where Are They Now?* and similar shows.

Then there is *Becoming*, which seems to take Warhol by his word, just as Kaufman did with the street singer at Carnegie Hall. Unlike Kaufman, however, this show does not even pretend to create stars in their own right. Turning ordinary fans into their favorite stars for the duration of one episode, *Becoming* promises to realize the democratization of stardom, while in fact, it only fabricates short-lived copies of already existing celebrities, and the show's openly ironic title offers a perfect example of how ideological discourses work. Clearly, everyone involved knows that the subjects of *Becoming* do not magically turn into their favorite celebrity in the process of the show, but still, the appearance that they do is maintained in the title. Though none of the second-hand stars on *Becoming* are deluded by this ideological promise, they still act as if someone else might mistake them for the real star instead of a copy. No wonder, then, that one of the most important issues in the show is often whether the subject's best friends are duped by the authenticity of his or her impersonation.[3]

Kaufman's array of show-business failures also featured a pre-emptive version of the second-degree stars that are serially produced by shows like *Becoming*. When he claimed that his Tony Clifton persona was just a copy of an original lounge singer he discovered in Las Vegas, Kaufman implicitly suggested that were it not for his own imitation of Tony Clifton, the supposedly real singer would never have become known at all. In a curious inversion, then, Kaufman anticipated the logic of *Becoming*, with the "original" Tony Clifton retroactively turning into a star because of Kaufman's impersonation.

Having said that, it is important to note that in most of his performances about failed stars, Kaufman's stance is not that of an overconformist performer of the American Dream. In the "Has-Been Corner" as well as in the case of the street singer at Carnegie Hall, the mode of Kaufman's critique of ideology is more conventional, as his strategy is clearly aimed at staging the repressed histories of failure that sustain the discourse of stardom. In these instances, Kaufman confronts his audience with the hidden truths of the cult of celebrity; hence his cultural-ideological criticism, while relying on an excessively literal interpretation of the American Dream, is aimed at an explicit exposure of what is obscured in its ideological promise of success.

The Most Authentic Wrestler

If routines like the "Has-Been Corner" illustrate what Philip Auslander calls Kaufman's "simultaneous exploitation and deconstruction of the cult of celebrity" (1992, 150), then Kaufman's career as a wrestler once again reveals him as the overconformist artist who relentlessly subjects himself to the ideological letter of the American Dream. If America guarantees its subjects the opportunity to live the dream of success and, by extension, to gain and enjoy the status of a celebrity, then Kaufman's "conversion" from comedian to wrestler represents his excessively literal enactment of this imaginary objective of the American Dream. Strictly operating within the coordinates of desire provided by the Dream, Kaufman enters the wrestling ring to fulfill this promise of stardom totally on his own account—and in such an orthodox way as to reveal the fundamental inconsistencies of the democracy of success implied by the American Dream.

At this point, it may be helpful to offer a brief outline of the crucial stages in Andy Kaufman's passage from comedy to wrestling. Basically, Kaufman's wrestling career may be split into two periods: first, his "intergender wrestling" acts, invariably involving women as his opponents and considered by Philip Auslander as the "most controversial performances" of Kaufman's entire career (145); second, Kaufman's interventions within professional wrestling, which culminated in his feud with wrestler Jerry Lawler in 1982. While the early fights usually occurred in Kaufman's comedy shows, or as integral parts of his guest appearances on television shows, his subsequent matches took place in the wrestling ring, which means that all the incidents that followed were contextually bound to the representational logic of professional wrestling.

The first time Kaufman performed his "intergender wrestling" routine on national television was on *The Tomorrow Show* on August 20, 1979. Kaufman's opponents at that time included a Playboy Bunny and two female staff members (Zehme 2001, 267), though usually he would recruit female volunteers from the audience, challenging them for a wrestling match "between the sexes." Eventually Kaufman "would claim to be undefeated in four hundred matches and to be the Intergender Wrestling Commission's recognized champion" (Auslander 1992, 146). Tossing around the most hackneyed of sexist stereotypes, he often adopted a strongly misogynistic stance in front of his increasingly hostile audience, which is one of the reasons why Auslander argues that intergender wrestling was "the most disturbing and, probably, the most obnoxious of Kaufman's performance gambits" (146). This reference to the act of wrestling women as "obnoxious" suggests that Kaufman's intergender wrestling shows structural aspects of perversion, and indeed, this part of his performance work is not about the enactment of that publicly acknowledged fantasy called the American Dream. There are more "intimate" issues of gender and sexual difference at stake here.

Incidentally, the notion of perversion is underscored by a statement from Kaufman himself, who is quoted saying that scuffling onstage with women was, quite simply, "a fantasy come true" (Zehme 2001, 209). If this suggests an explicitly sexual dimension to Kaufman's intergender wrestling, this same statement is also Kaufman's confession that these performance routines work according to the logic of perverse desire. A passage from Žižek's *The Plague of Fantasies* illustrates this perfectly well. Žižek describes the pervert as someone who enacts "a universe in which, as in cartoons, a human being can survive any catastrophe; in which adult sexuality is reduced to a childish game; in which one is not forced to die or to choose one of the two sexes" (1997, 34). Clearly, Kaufman's intergender wrestling represents the perfect example of a practice that reduces "adult sexuality" to a "childish game," as these playful, amateurish brawls trade the troublesome antagonism of real sexual encounters for the clear and simple situation of a one-on-one fight that has no real consequences. In this sense, Andy Kaufman's intergender wrestling routine constitutes an escape from the structural impossibility of sexual relations as captured by Lacan's famous dictum that "*il n'y a pas de rapport sexuel.*" After all, there is no deadlock in a wrestling match, and since the uncanny encounter with the other sex takes place in an imaginary combat zone, the antagonism of real sexual difference is projected onto the plain site of a children's game, and thereby reduced to a schoolyard fight.[4]

However, this is not to adopt the view of Kaufman's long-term collaborator Bob Zmuda, who argues that the entire concept of intergender wrestling is no more than a product of Kaufman's sexual fantasies. In the documentary section following the video of *Andy Kaufman Plays Carnegie Hall*, Zmuda claims that wrestling women "was totally Andy Kaufman's own sexual gratification." Based on the dirty joke that all of this was simply an enactment of the performer's private obsession with women, Zmuda implicitly denies Kaufman's intergender wrestling the status of a performance act proper, totally disregarding the extent to which these fights made a highly controversial social spectacle that fueled debates about gender politics. After all, wrestling women was not just another way of defying audience expectation, nor was it simply Kaufman's way of parodying professional wrestling. Transporting the spectacle of all-male wrestling into an explicitly heterosexual setting, these performances also obliquely articulate the strong sense of homosocial desire that underlies the blatant machismo displayed by professional wrestling.[5]

When Kaufman finally entered the ring of traditional "same-sex" wrestling, which was his most radical departure from the course of comedy, he disappeared from the radar of hip urban show-business culture. In their own way, though, Kaufman's interventions in the domain of professional wrestling turned into one of the most controversial acts of his entire performance history. More than just an investigation of the peculiar logic of this fictional sports spectacle, Kaufman's career in professional wrestling enacted, in the most orthodox fashion imaginable, the public fantasies of stardom represented by the American Dream. Arguably, wrestling designates the cultural arena where the mechanisms of show business and stardom are staged in the exaggerated form of caricature—and the most literal version of this is *Celebrity Deathmatch*, MTV's animated series featuring caricatured stars who engage in absurdly gory wrestling matches.

This notion of formal excess is also one of the key points of Roland Barthes's argument in his classic essay "The World of Wrestling," still one of the most concise reflections on the spectacle of wrestling. Although Barthes focuses on the French variant, his essay also applies to American wrestling, when, in the very first sentence, he defines wrestling as "the spectacle of excess" (1957, 15). Clearly, it should seem perfectly reasonable to describe wrestling as a spectacle that displays excess in terms of its representation of physical violence, but Barthes is less interested in actual bodies than in the *rhetorics* of wrestling. In his attempt to retheorize the notion of myth in semiological terms, he focuses on what he calls the "rhetorical amplification" of wrestling (23), an exaggeration that occurs in terms of signs and gestures. Accordingly, Barthes insists that "only the image is involved in the game, and the spectator does not wish for the actual suffering of the contestant; he only enjoys the perfection of an iconography" (20). If the spectacle of wrestling is to be read as a set of images to be perfected, then this may serve as a preliminary indication of how Andy Kaufman's performance work relates to professional wrestling. As the fundamentalist American Dreamer who enacts the public fantasies scripted by the American dream-ideology, Kaufman is also engaged in a project that is ultimately directed at the perfection of an iconography.

Kaufman's involvement with professional wrestling "officially" started on April 1, 1982, when he appeared on *Late Night with David Letterman*, announcing his match against Jerry "The King" Lawler, one of the most popular wrestlers at that time.[6] Four days later, the two unlikely combatants faced each other on the stage at the Mid-South Coliseum, Lawler's home stadium in Memphis. His appearance being ridiculously inadequate for a wrestler, Kaufman entered the ring and started to mock the audience, showing off his obvious lack of athletic skills. Inevitably, this illegitimate intruder from the domain of comedy provoked massive outrage among the wrestling community, and it was up to Jerry Lawler to act as the legitimate agency of punishment against this self-declared wrestler. As Kaufman's manager, George Shapiro, reports,

At the Mid-South Coliseum in Memphis, Andy Kaufman puts Jerry Lawler in a headlock, right before Lawler knocks him out with a piledriver. Still photograph taken from extra footage included on the *Man on the Moon* DVD (Universal Pictures, 1999).

Andy went into the ring at the Mid-South Coliseum to a tremendous chorus of boos. For the first five minutes after Andy went into the ring, he was dancing around, jumping around like a monkey, got out of the ring to protect himself, and after five minutes Jerry Lawler offered to let Andy put him in a headlock. So Andy got Lawler in a headlock. Lawler picked him up and threw him right on his back on the canvas. He hit pretty hard. Then Lawler grabbed him and gave him a piledriver, which is an illegal hold. . . . He did this twice. It looked like Andy's neck was broken. He was out for a couple of minutes. Then he woke in a lot of pain and the audience was hooting and cheering and really happy that Andy was hurt. (Quoted in Zehme 2001, 312)

Kaufman was carried out of the ring and taken to a hospital in an ambulance. But this was only the beginning of his involvement with the professional wrestling community.[7] Kaufman continued to attack Lawler verbally, insulting his Tennessee audience in a series of short promotional films, and eventually bringing the feud to national consciousness when he made another appearance on *Late Night with David Letterman*. This time, Lawler was with him when, on the segment that aired on July 28, 1982, Kaufman caused a veritable turmoil on the show. The incident made national news and thus reinforced the impression of an actual battle between Lawler and Kaufman.[8]

In fact, the spectacle of hatred between the two was a collaboration from the very start, but this knowledge was only integrated into "official history" when Jerry Lawler's coauthorship in the performance was eventually unmasked, more or less simultaneously, by *Man on the Moon*, Bill Zehme's biography *Lost in the Funhouse*, and Bob Zmuda's *Andy Kaufman Revealed!*. In their notes on the screenplay for *Man on the Moon*, Scott Alexander and Larry Karaszewski claim that right until the release of Forman's biopic, that is, for nearly two decades after these incidents, "people thought Andy and Lawler were huge enemies" (1999, 171). When Zmuda reveals that Lawler had been an accessory to the act from the start, he points out that the very first fight had already been perfectly choreographed and did not result in any real physical injury for Kaufman: "Jerry's pile driver was perfectly executed both times, leaving Andy completely unharmed" (Zmuda and Hansen 2001, 237). While it was true that Kaufman was hospitalized after the match, the diagnosis according to George Shapiro was that he suffered a mere "muscle strain" that was only so serious as to force Kaufman to wear a neck brace for a few days (Zehme 2001, 314). As Zehme adds, however, this slightest of injuries did not prevent Kaufman from wearing "the neck brace in public for the next five months" (314). In the guise of an injured wrestler, Kaufman continued his performance well beyond the actual fight.

Yet why does it matter if Kaufman's public feud with Jerry Lawler was entirely staged or not? Is it not common knowledge that the representational logic of wrestling is that of a scripted spectacle, with each and every move being part of an elaborate choreography? In what way, then, does an intruder like Kaufman undermine this logic, and in what way does his performance sustain the codes of wrestling as a fictional spectacle? Referring to David Marc, let me once again point out that (as discussed above) there is a significant analogy between professional wrestling and the performative stance taken by stand-up comedians. With wrestlers and stand-up comics alike, the audience is faced with the conflation of the performer's "face" and what appears to be his "mask." But unlike stand-up comedians, wrestlers are always recognizable as totally artificial characters—which is why the representational status of what takes place in the wrestling ring is not as precarious as it is in stand-up comedy. While a stand-up comedian wears his "face" as his "mask," this relation is inverted in wrestling. A

wrestler is all mask and no face, or more precisely, there is no performer behind the mask of a wrestler, because he simply does not
exist except in his role.[9]

In wrestling, the spectacle itself is acknowledged as a fictional artifice, and in this respect, professional wrestling differs
radically from Kaufman's "intergender" variant. When Kaufman
arranged onstage fights with female members from his comedy
audiences, none of them were ever choreographed beforehand.
In professional wrestling, on the other hand, the matches are all
scripted in advance, which is why Bill Zehme, in a passage that
adopts the point of view of young Andy Kaufman, describes wrestling as "a big lie, a phony deal, fabulous fakery probably kind of
all-made-up" (2001, 53). The notion of wrestling as a "big lie" is
misleading, though, because it suggests that the audience is actively
deceived with regard to what it sees. Quite on the contrary, the
crucial aspect about the representational logic of professional wrestling is not the fact that everything that happens in and around the
ring is staged, and a fiction—rather, the point is that the audience
knows that everything is a fiction.

Bob Zmuda provides a somewhat simplistic, yet concise description of the strange logic of this fictional spectacle, defining
wrestling as "a mutually agreed-upon fantasy between the participants and the viewers: we'll pretend to hurt each other, and you'll
pretend to believe it" (Zmuda and Hansen 2001, 56). In a more
scholarly jargon, Philip Auslander points out this curiously double-
edged logic when he describes wrestling as "a performance idiom
that is generally acknowledged to be fictional, even as its conventions always insist on its authenticity" (1992, 146). This ambivalence is reflected in wrestling terminology itself, as is neatly
illustrated by the binary opposition between the terms *work* and
shoot. According to the "Wrestling Glossary" (2000) published in
the *Pro-Wrestling On Line Museum*, the term *work* refers to "a

deception or sham," while the *shoot*, conversely, is defined as the "real thing" in the sense that "one participant is really attempting to hurt another." Hence, the terminology of wrestling acknowledges mere pretense as the ordinary by referring to it as *work*, but at the same time, the jargon perpetuates the authenticity of the fictional spectacle to the degree that it includes a term for the departure from the norm of pretense, namely, actual violence that causes real physical consequences. The paradox, then, is that the truly physical violence of a *shoot* is ruled out by the very logic of professional wrestling, which is acknowledged as fictional *work*.[10]

While the spectacle of wrestling is a highly manipulative form of theater, its manipulations are strictly part of the tacit contract between the contestants and the audience. Professional wrestling is based on this mutual consent to accept the pretense of a violent full-contact fight as what it is, namely, the mere *appearance* of a full-contact fight, and in this sense, this sports spectacle reads like a metaphor for ideology. Taking the most extreme example, Slavoj Žižek points out that under the Stalinist regime in the former Soviet Union, the rule of ideology was sustained by the peculiar logic that "it was not only forbidden to criticize Stalin, *it was perhaps even more forbidden to announce this very prohibition*" (1997, 28, italics in original). Though everyone knew that the regime was based on the prohibition of criticism, the *appearance* that criticism was in fact possible had to be maintained for the ideology to work. This same ideological mechanism of a "candid illusion" is at work in professional wrestling, where everyone involved is aware of the fact that every act of violence is just a pretense that does not cause any serious physical harm. At the same time, though, the appearance that real violence is possible needs to be maintained for the spectacle to be successful.

Hence, wrestling also demonstrates why ideology has nothing to do with a malign mechanism that produces delusional subjects.

One of the crucial points that Žižek has repeatedly stressed is the seeming paradox that in ideology the subject need not be actively deceived about the true state of things in order for the ideological discourse to work. On the contrary, ideology works best if the subjects keep a certain "objective" distance—and wrestling serves as a perfect illustration for this point. Although the wrestling audience is fully aware of the fictional status of the spectacle they witness, their immersion in the game suggests an emotional investiture that would seem totally unreasonable to the detached observer. But how do we explain this?

In his book *Die Illusionen der anderen*, Robert Pfaller has offered an intriguing theoretical concept for this kind of problem.[11] Noting that we often act according to superstitious ideas that we would not call our own, Pfaller has raised the question if "there are illusions that always belong to others, without ever being anyone's own illusions" (2002, 11, my translation). For example, he asks, why is it that reasonable, civilized people are compelled to talk to their car if the ignition fails to start, even though they know perfectly well that this kind of metaphysical incantation is pointless in the face of technology? For Pfaller, situations like this one suggest that we are prone to a curious kind of "civilized" magic that we know fully well is pure superstition. In fact, one may assume that no one ever believed in these illusions, and this is why Pfaller terms this type of superstitions as "illusions without owners," or, "illusions without subjects."

The crucial point about these illusions without owners is that they are not only *not* dismissed by the fact that we actually know better, but it is by our better knowledge that these illusions are established in the first place. Drawing on Johan Huizinga's theory of the play element in culture, Pfaller then points out that our fascination with games has nothing to do with forgetting about the illusion and mistaking the game for the real thing. On the contrary, he argues, "it is only when we see through the illusion of the game that we are captured by this illusion" (115, my translation). This explains why the fascination of wrestling is not undermined by the fact that the audience knows that the apparent violence in the ring is not real. As the seemingly paradoxical logic of Huizinga's theory teaches us, it is precisely the "objective" distance gained from this knowledge which allows for their massive emotional investment in the game.

Accordingly, the pleasure of watching wrestling depends on the curious logic that it is always the *others* who are duped by the appearance of actual violence. The illusion is assigned to imaginary believers, and in the shooting script for *Man on the Moon*, the Lawler character implicitly acknowledges this logic of enjoyment, stating that he would not have traded the feud with Kaufman for anything: "Because for one brief, shining moment . . . the world thought that wrestling was real" (Alexander and Karaszewski 1999, 111). This line is not included in the film, but it neatly illustrates why Pfaller's notion of "illusions without owners" is so perfectly appropriate to describe the peculiar fascination of this sports spectacle. What is essential for the pleasure of the wrestling community is that the *world* (not the audience) is caught up in the belief that wrestling matches are actual full-contact fights. On the other hand, if the wrestling audience was caught up in the belief that the violence displayed is real, the ideological distance that enables them to identify with the spectacle in the first place would be shattered.[12]

One might argue that once Andy Kaufman stepped into the wrestling ring, the sheer inferiority of his physical presence made this distance collapse. Was it not the case that Kaufman, once again being literally displaced, as a comedian, inscribed the possibility of real violence into professional wrestling, thereby bringing the entire spectacle to the test? While it may seem that he "ridiculed professional wrestling," as Jerry Lawler states in the documentary *I'm from Hollywood* (1989), the point is that Kaufman's interventions did not shatter the symbolic framework of wrestling at all. If his wrestling performances questioned the codes of the spectacle, they did so in a way that strictly conformed to its implicit doctrine.

In one of his crucial arguments from "The World of Wrestling," Roland Barthes points out that "the function of the wrestler is not to win; it is to go exactly through the motions which are expected of him" (1957, 16). But if the wrestler's function is to avoid the unexpected by faithfully reproducing the motions required by the code of the spectacle, this function gets precarious in the French type of the *bastard*. Essentially an unstable character "who accepts the rules only when they are useful to him and transgresses the formal continuity of attitudes," the bastard, according to Barthes, "is unpredictable, therefore asocial" (24). As Barthes makes clear, the bastard enrages the audience not simply because he violates the symbolic laws on which the spectacle is based, but rather, the scandal arises due to the bastard's sheer inconsistency with respect to these laws, so the audience is "offended not in its morality but in its logic" (24). Thus, this type of character seems to mark a crisis point within the code of the spectacle, because the bastard's presence introduces the possibility of unexpectedness into a spectacle ruled by the principle of perfectly fulfilled expectation. Within the highly encoded world of wrestling, which is based upon the very prohibition of unexpected moves, the bastard incorporates the institutionalized exception to that rule. But since the transgressive inconsistency of his motions is directed against the symbolic laws of wrestling, the bastard is yet another example of the inherent transgressor, whose violations represent just that force of transgression that effectively serves to sustain the spectacle and reinforce its laws.

It must be said at this point that Barthes insists on a fundamental difference between French and American wrestling, which is that the characters in the French variant are based on ethical concepts, whereas American wrestling characters are created according to quasi-political binary oppositions between good and evil. Still, the American mode features a type that corresponds to the French bastard in the sense that he also implements institutionalized transgressions. This is the *heel*, the proverbial "bad guy" of wrestling who often cheats and does not respect the rules. As a former comedian who invaded the domain of wrestling by his own right, Andy Kaufman clearly cast himself in the character of the heel from the very start, and the way he insulted and mocked the entire wrestling community in Tennessee indicates just how consistently he performed his role as the villain.

Within his character, Kaufman strictly acted according to the formal codes of wrestling, and only once did his performance seem to exceed the conventions of a heel's code of conduct. This was when Kaufman offered Jerry Lawler the opportunity to join forces in order to beat another team, though as soon as the unlikely alliance had entered the ring, Kaufman turned against his new partner, suggesting a form of inconsistency similar to the attitude that Barthes ascribes to the French bastard. Kaufman had already shown this kind of inconsistent behavior during the negotiations before that particular fight, when he offered Lawler $10,000 if he agreed to join forces—the very same check that he had previously offered as a reward for any wrestler who would send Lawler to the hospital.

However, none of this is evidence enough that Kaufman might have imported the ethical inconsistency of the French bastard into American wrestling, because even his seemingly rueful effort to reconcile with Lawler (only to stab him in the back once they were in the ring) is already prefigured within the American code of the spectacle. In the vocabulary of wrestling, the technical term for this kind of conversion is *turn*, referring to the moment when a heel switches his persona to play a *face* and become a "good guy." Pretending to prepare for a turn, Kaufman was simply a heel performing an elaborate ruse to double-cross the face. In this sense, Kaufman's treacherous act against his supposed ally was not at all a violation of the formal logic of the spectacle—on the contrary, it was an effect of Kaufman's most faithful enactment of that very logic.

Ultimately, then, the crucial point about Kaufman's career in professional wrestling is that once he had entered the ring, he never betrayed the logic of the spectacle, but he conformed to the laws of American wrestling even when he seemed to transgress them. If there was anything outrageous about these performances, it was not that Kaufman might have shattered the "candid illusion" of wrestling, nor was it the simple fact that the hip urban comedian was so ridiculously out of place within the wrestling arena in the south. What was truly outrageous about Kaufman performing as a wrestler was the fact that he perfectly fulfilled the requirements of the spectacle. As he relentlessly insisted on the authenticity of the fights and his feud with Lawler, his performances were totally consistent with the implicit doctrine of this fictional spectacle, and this is why Kaufman truly represents the most authentic wrestler one could imagine. Conversely, it was the supposedly "authentic" wrestler Jerry Lawler who, when finally confessing to the fictional status of his feud with Kaufman, acted against the code of wrestling. Hence, the ex-comedian curiously turns out to be more orthodox in terms of professional wrestling than the real wrestler himself.

Two possible conclusions can be drawn here. First, Kaufman's wrestling career could be read as another act of the over-conformist artist. According to this reading, his performances as a wrestler would support the point that maybe it is more subversive to hold on to the ideological letter against the ideology itself (in this case, to insist on the authenticity of wrestling) than to unmask the ideological discourse (to publicly state that wrestling is a charade and a fictional theater, which is pointless because everyone knows that it is). The second possible conclusion is much simpler, and it brings me back to the American Dream as a democratic promise that makes stardom accessible to every American subject. In the end, maybe the single most scandalous thing about Kaufman's interventions in the wrestling ring was the fact that he took this promise to its literal extremes.

The Self-Made Star

One of the most striking features about the way Kaufman's wrestling performances are documented in *I'm from Hollywood* is the prevalence of the notion of fantasy. When supposed adversary Jerry Lawler identifies the central issue of Kaufman's conversion from comedian to wrestler, he points out Kaufman's desire to fulfill his dreams and "to live out his fantasy of being a wrestler." Stating that he is determined to end these dreams, Lawler addresses Kaufman in the film, expressing his threat that "it will be the last time that you fantasize about being a wrestler."

However, if Lawler insists that a wrestling career was "just Andy's way of living out his fantasies," this should not be mistaken as another indication of perverse desire. If there is something perverse about Kaufman's performances in the domain of professional wrestling, it is because the structure of perversion is inscribed in the spectacle itself. After all, does not wrestling represent just the kind of "cartoon universe" that the pervert, according to Slavoj Žižek, tries to enact? Regardless of the excessive violence that the opponents are suffering, the brutal spectacle of wrestling takes place in a symbolic realm where the protagonists can "survive any catastrophe" and are indeed "not forced to die." Hence, if Kaufman displays elements of perversion in his performance as a wrestler, then this is the perversion inherent in wrestling.

When Kaufman joins this spectacle, it is less the enactment of a secret fantasy of his than it is a literal version of the fantasies about stardom and celebrity that lie at the heart of America's social imaginary—in short, what is at stake here is the democracy of success as articulated in the American dream-ideology. When Jerry Lawler refers to Kaufman's controversial involvement with professional wrestling as "just Andy's way of living out his fantasies," the alleged fantasies we are dealing with here are those that define Kaufman as the true subject of the public discourse that is the American Dream. This is not to say that the ideology of the Dream summons its subjects to become stars specifically in the wrestling ring, but Kaufman's wrestler persona must be read as a metonymy for any cultural practice that holds the American promise of stardom. If the American subject is defined by the democratic opportunity to become a star, then why should you not reinvent yourself and become a wrestler, even if you do not seem to meet the physical requirements for the wrestling ring?

What is crucial is that Kaufman becomes a wrestling star simply because he acts like one, and arguably, it is this truly performative act that constitutes the most provocative aspect of his wrestler persona. In *Stars*, Richard Dyer discusses the ambiguities of the American democracy of stardom, and one of the major questions, he argues, "is whether success is possible for anyone, regardless of talent or application" (1998, 42). This is exactly what is at stake in Andy Kaufman's entire wrestling career, revealing once again his truly literalist stance with respect to the American myth of success: If there are no social frontiers whatsoever that regulate the democratic distribution of success, then he (or anyone) may as well declare himself the "World's Intergender

Wrestling Champion," or a professional wrestling star. Ultimately, this is the radical ambiguity within the American story of success that is articulated in Kaufman's conversion from comedian to wrestler.

Quoting the title of Joshua Gamson's study of American celebrity culture (1994), I would argue that Kaufman realizes the *claims to fame* that are inscribed in the American Dream about the "myth of success"—and what is probably even more scandalous, he fulfills its promise totally in his own account. Kaufman does not even bother about the appearance of being somehow "elected" by the mysterious mechanisms of fame. He takes the "freedom to become a star" not as what it is (an empty ideological gesture to be rejected), but he understands this freedom literally, as a freedom to be taken. Once again, Kaufman troubled America's social imaginary by enacting, in an excessively literal way, another portion of the public fantasy represented by the American Dream.

Finally, there is a crucial point about the fact that Kaufman specifically chose the domain of wrestling to enact the promise of stardom. Professional wrestlers are those entertainers whose immortality is most explicitly perpetuated in the practice of their performance. The very logic of their performance work allows wrestlers to suffer lethal injuries and yet always to return. Wrestling enacts a cartoon universe in which a human being can survive any violent attack and is still not forced to die—and in this sense, wrestling is truly the caricatured spectacle of immortal stars. In the mode of excess, wrestlers incorporate the image of immortality that lies at the core of the notion of stardom.

Epitaph

Immortality, not death, becomes the ultimate horror.

—Slavoj Žižek, *The Ticklish Subject*

Andy Kaufman Plays Carnegie Hall (1979) features what was probably Kaufman's most insidious presentation on how intricately fame and stardom are linked to death. Following the projection of "Mary-Ann," an obscure promotional short film from the early 1930s, Kaufman welcomes an old lady whom he introduces as Eleanor Cody Gould, claiming that she is the last survivor from the ensemble of cowgirls that were dancing in the film. After a brief and somewhat whimsical conversation, Kaufman has her (supposedly original) hobbyhorse brought onstage, and he asks the sole "survivor" to perform her cowgirl's dance once again. Old Mrs. Gould agrees to do so, and as she starts dancing the same piece that we have seen in the promotional short from nearly half a century ago, Andy Kaufman acts as the musical director of the live band; the musicians are playing "I've Got Spurs That Jingle Jangle Jingle," but as Kaufman is leading them to a gradual acceleration, Mrs. Gould appears to have trouble keeping up with the rhythm. Soon the conductor has his orchestra play so fast as to cause the aged dancer to collapse with what seems to be a heart attack, and right on center stage she falls to the ground, dying in front of the audience.

On the videotape of the show, all that can be heard now are some scattered laughs from the auditorium, then there is a brief silence, as if from shock or embarrassment. For a short while, nothing happens, until Bob Zmuda appears on the stage to ask if there happens to be a doctor present. On stage, some rather half-hearted attempts are made to bring the motionless dancer back to life, and by now the audience appears to be rapt in dead silence. As the efforts to reanimate the dancer do not seem to be successful, her body is eventually covered with a jacket, which supposedly signals the death of the old lady. Her corpse is left alone on an otherwise empty stage, until Andy Kaufman finally takes the stage again. Dressed as an Indian shaman, he dances around dead Mrs. Gould; as if by magic, he succeeds in bringing her back to life, and the cowgirl's death is comfortably revealed as a travesty.

If this scene reads like a commentary on the intricacies of death and stardom, what is particularly significant is the way in which Andy Kaufman "kills off" Mrs. Gould before resurrecting her. Bringing the last surviving cowgirl back from oblivion, Kaufman forces the old lady to compulsively repeat the image that signifies her single brush with celebrity, her long-forgotten one-time appearance on celluloid; re-enacting the scene of her own few minutes of fame, she is driven to perform the dance at ever higher speed. Thus, her "star identity" is tied to some sort of an automotive merry-go-round that eventually turns deadly due to sheer speed. In the end, Mrs. Gould's "death" is caused by the compulsion to endlessly live through this faint and distant moment of fame.

If Kaufman's musical acceleration kills the cowgirl, this means that she dies of being fatally caught up in her own past as in a historical loop, but by the time she is finally reanimated after her feigned death, the physical "survivor" has been resurrected as a survivor of a different order. Previously, when Mrs. Gould entered the stage, she was introduced as a survivor simply in biological terms, since she was the only person who happened to be still alive from the cast of a short film lost in oblivion. When she finally leaves the stage, however, she has turned into a "symbolic" survivor of what we have witnessed as the deadly roundabout of show business.

This episode with the un-dying cowgirl at Carnegie Hall is only one of numerous acts that saw Kaufman dealing with issues of mortality, or actually performing a scene of dying. At closer inspection, Kaufman's entire career seems to be haunted by a preoccupation with death, and, more specifically, with suicidal gestures performed in public. Bill Zehme's biography is crammed with references to Kaufman's alleged obsession with dying and, every now and then, people are mentioned who remember Kaufman performing his own death in some way or another, or stating his wish to do so.[1] For instance, Zehme quotes one Burt Dubrow, a fellow student of Kaufman's at the Cambridge School of Business in Boston, who reports that in the late 1960s, Kaufman threatened to shoot himself in the head on a television program that aired on the school's own WCSB-TV station. Dubrow hosted the show, and according to his recollection, Kaufman presented himself as the failed comedian who feels maltreated by his ignorant audience that would not laugh at him, and "after crying crying crying, he reached into his pocket and pulled out a gun! Then he put the gun to his head and just as he was going to shoot himself, I ran over and tackled him to the ground and—commercial!" (2001, 115). Kaufman would execute this kind of suicidal gesture again in February 1972. Hired as the opening act for the Temptations in Northampton, Massachusetts, Kaufman performed a suicide that was specifically designed as "punishment" for his audience.

> The predominantly black audience was, according to [Kaufman's] subsequent reports, completely offput by Foreign Man and made it

> vociferously known and so he wept and wept onstage and pulled out
> his large cap gun and walked off into the wings and fired the gun
> into a microphone and thudded to the floor and the room went
> silent and the Temptations sang extra hard that night to make up
> for it. (Zehme 2001, 131)

Finally, the most illustrative account of Kaufman's early death performances comes from Gil Gevins, who knew Kaufman from his
teenage years in his native Great Neck, Long Island, when they
were both members of a hippie-like clique called the F Troop.
Remembering a "show" that the F Troop performed at the home
of one of the members, Gevins tells Zehme how Andy Kaufman,
among other acts, sang "The House of the Rising Sun," at the end
of which

> he pretended to die—and die—and die. "He died for fifteen min-
> utes," said Gevins. "Like he'd been shot in one place, goes down,
> gets to his knees, he's shot in another place, he gets up, he's writhing
> on the ground again, he gets up, goes down . . . then up . . . then
> down—for *fifteen minutes!* . . . It was like a precursor to Andy's
> whole career in microcosm." (78, italics in original)

Incidentally, Gevins' account of Kaufman feigning his death for
fifteen minutes once again evokes Andy Warhol, for it makes
young Andy Kaufman's struggle "not to die" seem like an allegory
of what Warhol would call everybody's fifteen minutes of fame—
after all, the most basic definition of the star is that he is someone
who outlives himself in his own image as a cultural icon. Clearly,
this recollection of some teenage party should not be overrated,
but the crucial point is that it involves a process of recoding
Kaufman. If any particular act is experienced as if it prefigured an
entire career "in microcosm," then its very status as supposed

"precursor" can never be established by any other way than from a belated point in history.

Jacques Lacan's notion of the *point de capiton* is helpful here, because in Lacanian terms, the operation that Gevins performs in his account is he designates this particular biographical event as the "quilting point" for Kaufman's entire body of work. As Dylan Evans states in his *Introductory Dictionary of Lacanian Psychoanalysis*, what Lacan terms the *point de capiton* refers to the place where the endless movement of signification is stopped in order to make possible the emergence of "the necessary illusion of a fixed meaning" (2001, 149). By implication, the structure of this quilting point is both synchronic as well as diachronic, as with the meaning of the first words in a sentence, which is only determined retroactively when the sentence is completed.

In this sense, the particular biographical detail of young Andy Kaufman pretending to die for fifteen minutes is transformed into a metaphor for his entire history as a performer, but this metaphoric precursor can only be established by means of a retroactive gesture after the trajectory of Kaufman's career is completed, in an attempt to arrest the continuous flow of signifiers. Ultimately, then, what Gevins proposes is just a slightly more refined version of the Rosebud that the screenwriters for *Man on the Moon* could not find in Kaufman's history as an entertainer.

Perhaps one could also read the desire to mark this *point de capiton* in Kaufman's biography as an indication that he caused some sort of psychotic experience among the American public. After all, here is an entertainer who takes literally the ideological injunctions of the American Dream, and thus displays the structural features of a true psychotic. As Slavoj Žižek points out in *The Ticklish Subject*, a madman is someone who "confuses the order of 'words' and the order of 'things,' which, precisely, is the most elementary and succinct definition of psychosis" (1999, 274). Is this not also true for Kaufman, who mistakes the ideological imperative of the American Dream for some sort of a "biographical manual" to be enacted in the real, thereby confusing the "word" of ideology with an actual "thing"?

Still, I would like to replace the notion of Kaufman as a psychotic subject with the thesis that he was a performer who effectively produced an *American spectacle of psychosis*—a disturbing theatre whose psychotic structure is prescribed, or scripted, by the American Dream. To resume the argument about the desire to capture the essence of Kaufman's work by establishing a quilting point in his biography, let me refer to Dylan Evans once again. If the structure of psychosis is defined by a "lack of sufficient *points de capiton*," he notes, this entails "that the psychotic experience is characterised by a constant slippage of the signified under the signifier, which is a disaster for signification" (2001, italics in original). The notion of a disastrous effect on signification may recall Hal Foster's concept of the traumatic "failure to signify" that marks the event of the avant-garde, but the disaster of signification inherent in the psychotic experience is of a different order. In psychosis, signification does not fail in a moment of trauma, but it fails because the signifier is being continuously reshaped.

This is exactly what the American public experienced in the face of the "signifier" that was Andy Kaufman. Here was a performer in the entertainment business who failed to "make sense" precisely because he underwent continuous reshaping in a most radical sense. As a serial subject, Kaufman *embodied* a chain of signifiers, which made it impossible to stop the movement of endless signification. Of course, though, the crucial point is that this seemingly inconsistent process of permanent transformation is a necessary effect of the predominant public discourse that is the American Dream. In his absolute compliance with its imperative,

Kaufman produced a spectacle of psychosis in the sense that he confronted the American public with the inconsistent kernel of their publicly acknowledged fantasies as represented in the ideological text of the American Dream.

Renata Salecl, when defining psychosis, focuses on the relation of the psychotic experience to the constitutive stain that needs to be precluded to render consistency to the screen of reality. In psychosis, she writes, this stain "materializes itself, it receives full bodily presence and becomes visible" (1994, 106). Now, if every ideological discourse can only function on the condition that it obfuscates some inherent "stain" that would otherwise undermine its consistency, then what I would argue is precluded in the American Dream is the traumatic recognition of failure and, ultimately, mortality. In the theatre of Andy Kaufman, however, this stain receives full bodily presence, and in the last instance, this is what renders it an American spectacle of psychosis. As a result of his absolute identification with the letter of the American Dream, Kaufman brings to light its fundamental inconsistency with regard to death.

"Simply an Act": Andy Kaufman and Lacanian Ethics

If the scene of young Andy Kaufman dying for fifteen minutes may be interpreted as a metaphoric "precursor" for Kaufman's career as a performer, what are the implications of designating it as the *point de capiton* for his work? The first thing to note here is that within the genre of stand-up comedy, a scene like this is structurally impossible. According to John Limon, there is absolutely no room for an act of "dying" on the stage of stand-up comedy, and even if there is the occasional exception, it only confirms the rule. For example, when discussing a comedy concert where Richard Pryor pretends to have a heart attack at one point during a show, Limon points out that this act constitutes a singular moment in the history of stand-up comedy: "There is nothing like it in all of stand-up, which almost by definition cannot permit falling down" (2000, 87). For stand-up comedians, the very signifier of dying is invariably an index of being rejected by their audience, and therefore the specter of the comedian's death must be excluded by all accounts, because it would be equivalent with the complete failure of making the audience laugh.

Conversely, stand-up comedians may be "killed" by the audience's rejection, as is the case with the protagonist at the beginning of *Funny Bones*, when his debut in Las Vegas turns into a traumatic experience of public failure. As the audience is empowered to execute this "symbolic death" at any given time, the stand-up comedian, more than any other stage performer, is haunted by an immense fear of dying. This is very neatly illustrated by the Lenny Bruce character in Don DeLillo's novel *Underworld*, who addresses his audience with the words: "Love me unconditionally or I die. These are the terms of our engagement" (1997, 582). In this sense, Andy Kaufman truly did put his life more radically at risk than any other performer within the genre of stand-up. Facing audiences who are conditioned to laugh, he risked his "death" simply because he tended to stretch their patience up to the point of exhaustion, thereby testing the terms of their engagement. Quoting an article from *New York* magazine, Bill Zehme notes that Kaufman "is simply not afraid to die" (2001, 221). Yet there is more to this aspect of Kaufman's work than the fact that dying on stage did not seem to scare him.[2]

In his truly suicidal gestures, Kaufman's designs to exhaust the patience of his audience were often structured so as to seduce them into actually "killing" him. As Bob Zmuda points out, Kaufman would refer to these acts of self-destruction as his "bombing routine," which meant that "he would go onstage and cause to happen what every comic who's ever lived fears most: the complete failure to get a laugh" (Zmuda and Hansen 2001, 57). As I have made clear above, Kaufman engaged in these willful self-immolations from early on in his career, but in his later years, they gained an unprecedented poignancy.

In 1982 an unshaven, distraught and disheveled Andy Kaufman was a guest on David Letterman's short-lived morning show on NBC, talking about *Taxi* and finally delivering a long monologue about the divorce he claimed to have gone through; apparently suffering from a severe cough, Kaufman eventually begged for money, panhandling among the audience until he was escorted out by security guards.[3] Gerard Mulligan, a coordinator for the show and subsequently a writer for *Late Night with David Letterman*, recalls Kaufman's ideas about how to end this scene of a star's public self-degradation. As Mulligan points out, Kaufman "wanted to take out a prop gun and shoot himself in the head. He said he had always wanted to do that on television" (Zehme 2001, 286). The following three episodes will illustrate just how radical and consistent Kaufman was in his various acts of suicidal behavior, and what their implications are in terms of the uncanny kernel that haunts the American Dream.

Chronologically speaking, the first instance of Kaufman taking his "bombing routine" beyond the context of comedy occurred on September 13, 1979, when he held a press conference in San Francisco in order to promote his forthcoming show at Harrah's Casino in Las Vegas. According to Bob Zmuda, Kaufman saw his integrity as a performer being questioned when a journalist accused him on a number of charges, starting with the disclosure that various guest stars from his Carnegie Hall show had in fact been considerably less glamorous stand-ins (members of the Olga Fricker School of Dance doubling for the Radio City Music Hall Rockettes, and the Manhattan City Choir standing in for the Mormon Tabernacle Choir). The reporter continued his tirade for some time, also addressing more intimate topics, until eventually he was ejected by a publicist from Harrah's Casino (Zmuda and Hansen 2001, 153–56).

In fact, while these literally defaming accusations were all correct, the anonymous journalist who publicly denounced Kaufman was none other than Kaufman's collaborator Bob Zmuda, playing the part of a news reporter among the press people. It may be impossible to retrospectively determine if the journalists present were actually duped by this charade, but the crucial point about the scene is not the question of who was fooled or who was not. What truly matters here is the fact that this performance was no longer simply a "conceptualist" exercise in not getting a laugh. On a relatively small scale, this was Kaufman's prologue for more substantial acts that put his social existence in show business dramatically at risk.[4]

This episode was followed by even more radical acts of self-induced destruction, and though both incidents took place within the domain of comedy, neither of them was a stand-up "suicide" in terms of a comedian's failure to make the audience laugh. Arguably, Kaufman's most ingenious suicidal gesture dates from 1982, when he was invited to feature on a comedy special taped by HBO, celebrating the tenth anniversary of the Catch a Rising Star club. Having been repeatedly criticized for his lack of new comic material, Kaufman now went so far as to openly stage this very lack of new comedy routines and turn it into the premise for his performance on the *Catch a Rising Star's 10th Anniversary* (1982). As Zehme dramatically phrases it, this was where Kaufman "decided to kill it off, to put the material out of its misery, to expose it as the charade and the lodestone that it had become" (2001, 323). Again, the idea was that Bob Zmuda should bring Kaufman into disrepute, only this time the strategy was not to accuse him of dishonest entertainment practices but to actively disrupt his popular Foreign Man performance by anticipating the entire act word by word—suggesting that Kaufman's Foreign Man act was so well known by then that anyone from the audience might be able to quote every line before it was even uttered on the stage. "And this was not mere heckling," Bill Zehme writes about this doubled performance, "it was worse and also better; it was the act anticipated, performed in parsed phrases, slightly ahead of itself. It was Foreign Man unmasked and torched and vanquished forever" (2001, 324). Explicitly staging the effect of a general overfamiliarity with Kaufman's Foreign Man persona, the scene exposed the widespread idea that audiences had long grown weary of the character.[5]

However, the scene did not end at this point, for Zmuda finally unmasked himself, announcing that the entire scene of his degradation was part of the script. Like a claqueur in reverse, Zmuda confessed that he was expressly hired to heckle Kaufman, which means that ultimately what is exposed in the act is exposure itself, and the subversive gesture is subverted in turn.[6] Referring to this scene as "the disemboweling of an actual life and career," Bill Zehme draws attention to the vicissitudes of truth and fiction that are at work in this act, arguing that "whether or not what was happening was real, it was nevertheless all very true and all very profoundly true" (325). Not only is Foreign Man "vanquished forever," but in a curious fashion, the heckler's insolent interruptions are retroactively legitimized as soon as Zmuda identifies himself, because once he is revealed as part of the act, it is no longer possible for the audience to sympathize with the supposedly unnerved Kaufman who seems to be on the verge of "dying" on the stage of stand-up comedy. The moment Zmuda discloses his identity, every one of his accusations about Kaufman's performance prove correct: It is true that Kaufman has no new comedy routines, it is true that people know Foreign Man's lines by heart, and so on.

Paradoxically, then, it is only when the troublemaker is identified as an accessory to the act that his previous accusations turn out to be the truth about Kaufman. In other words, the fictional character is accepted as the speaker of the truth only after he has revealed himself as fictional, and the destructive gesture involved in this performance is all the more effective for being exposed as self-induced.[7]

That same year, Kaufman prepared what would turn out as his most radical act of embracing his own death. It started on November 13, 1982, when Dick Ebersol, executive producer of *Saturday Night Live*, read an official statement in the show, the purpose of which was to explain why Kaufman, who had been scheduled to appear as a special guest a few weeks earlier, was cut from two previous segments of the show. According to Bob Zmuda, Ebersol's speech was greeted with applause from the studio audience as he expressed his opinion that "Andy Kaufman is not funny anymore" (2001, 248). Clearly, this sanctioning statement from one of the father-figures of *Saturday Night Live* recalls the paternal lesson that the protagonist in *Funny Bones* takes from Jerry Lewis, but contrary to the way things turn out in Peter Chelsom's film, Kaufman did not accept the paternal death sentence from Ebersol. Determined to turn this public denouncement of filial insufficiency into what Zehme calls "a monstrosity of consumptive rejection" (2001, 331), the punished son arranged his own trial, as Kaufman called for a vote that would enable the audience of *Saturday Night Live* to decide if he should be allowed to return—or be banished from the show forever.

A week after Ebersol's public statement, a tele-vote was taken to decide Kaufman's fate. The idea was modeled on an earlier segment of the show from the previous year, when Eddie Murphy, having a lobster ready to be cooked on live television, asked the audience to decide if the animal (nicknamed Larry the Lobster) should live or end in the pot. In terms of audience participation, the statistics were already disappointing for Kaufman, as his poll drew considerably fewer participants than Murphy's, with a total of 364,730 votes as opposed to 466,548 viewers who called in the case of the Larry the Lobster. But the actual outcome was even more devastating. While the crustacean had been saved by the democratic poll among the television community of *Saturday Night Live*, Kaufman lost his case by 169,186 to 195,544 votes, and as a result of his own terms, he was effectively banned from the show, never to return before he died a year and a half later.

Clearly, these were the consequences of Kaufman's literal enactment of the "democracy of stardom" implied in the American Dream. If everyone has the democratic right to become a star, then the people should have the right to vote a star off the stage of success. According to Zehme, Kaufman was fully aware that he was likely to be voted out, and he was even looking forward to his own death sentence on *Saturday Night Live:* "He knew he would lose. He told Zmuda. He told George" (2001, 332). Zmuda, for his part, observes that finally Kaufman's "desire to succeed at failure had come full circle" in this poll, but he also insists on some sort of a conspiracy theory according to which Kaufman only risked the vote on the condition of a "secret agreement" with Dick Ebersol (2001, 250–51). According to this oral contract, Zmuda claims, Kaufman should still be allowed to return on the show in the guise of Tony Clifton.

Leaving aside the question if Kaufman did in fact foresee his own defeat or not, the crucial point about the entire episode was that Kaufman was determined to put everything at stake, as he engaged in a radical gesture of potential self-destruction. Against the backdrop of this kind of suicidal behavior, one particular remark from Lorne Michaels suggests a compelling allegiance linking Kaufman's work to Lacanian theory. Recalling the first time he saw Kaufman on stage, the creator of *Saturday Night Live* points out: "Aside from being funny, he wasn't enmeshed in the show business of it—show business being simply an act. There seemed to be some other commitment, something very pure and more personal about what he was doing" (cited in Zehme 2001, 156). Adopting Kaufman's literalist stance and taking these words more literally than they are intended, I would propose to turn this statement upside down and read it more radically in terms of Lacanian psychoanalysis. If Lorne Michaels suggests that Kaufman's show business was not "simply an act" in the common sense of illusion and mere pretense, then in terms of Lacanian ethics, Kaufman's business was precisely to engage in a series of *acts*. Considering the three "suicidal" performances related above, the supposed "purity" of Kaufman's commitment resides in the fact that his acts are in fact genuinely *ethical acts* in terms of Lacan's *Seminar VII*.

As Slavoj Žižek points out in *The Ticklish Subject*, to perform an authentic *acte* in the sense of Lacan is to "court" and "pursue" death in a gesture to risk one's entire social identity (1999, 263). Clearly, this serves as an exact description of what is ultimately at stake in Kaufman's performances of self-immolation. The scripted accusations at the press conference in San Francisco, the willful destruction of Foreign Man, clearly the most popular of his various personae, and most poignantly, offering the audience of *Saturday Night Live* to ban him from the show for all times to come—in each of these gestures, Kaufman increasingly "courts" and "pursues" his own death, putting at risk his very existence as an entertainer. What we have here is not just a comedian who "dies" again and again because his jokes fail to produce laughter, but here is a performer who repeatedly puts at stake his social position within the symbolic network of show business. The crucial point about these publicly staged gestures of suicide is that they are in fact necessary effects of Kaufman's literalist stance regarding the American Dream.

As I have already made clear, one of the central paradoxes of the discursive structure of the American Dream consists in the fact that its two basic vectors prove fundamentally incompatible. Complying with the ideological injunction to constantly reinvent oneself would result in a frantic activity of refashioning the self that renders impossible the very object of the promise, namely, enjoyment. However, an even more fundamental inconsistency inherent in the American Dream concerns the way death is hidden in its ideological imperative. As a protective fiction that offers an escape from the traumatic recognition of mortality, the American Dream conceals the fact that it only works at the expense of a series of small deaths.

This is precisely what is articulated in Andy Kaufman's willful acts of self-immolation. What may seem to be merely one entertainer's private obsession with suicidal gestures is in fact a necessary effect of the American Dream, as Kaufman's "bombing routine" enacts the uncanny flipside of the limitless possibility of refashioning oneself. Within the sequential logic of the myth of success, what is obscured in the letter of the American Dream is the fact that with every new version of yourself, the previous one is dismissed, or sentenced to death. Ultimately, the "happy" serial subjects produced by the American Dream are subjects that serially kill themselves.[8]

This is the radical ambiguity at the heart of this public fantasy, and, intriguingly, it persists even in those star biographies where the myth of success appears to be "successfully" realized. Within the ideological framework of the American Dream, an immortal body can only be had on the condition that another body dies—and this is best illustrated in terms of how Andy Kaufman relates to Elvis Presley.

Elvis Is (Not) Dead

At first sight, any alleged analogy between Andy Kaufman and Elvis Presley may seem to rest merely on the evidence that one of Kaufman's most popular routines was his exquisite impersonation of Elvis. It has often been stated that Kaufman was one of the most celebrated among the vast number of imitators that Presley has inspired to this day, and in his shows his imitation of Elvis invariably constituted that moment when the "failure" in terms of "regular" stand-up comedy impressions was superseded by a triumphant act of mimesis. Arguably, the most remarkable example is found in *The Midnight Special* (1981), where Foreign Man's deliberately poor impersonations of Ronald Reagan and Steve Martin segue into an impeccable Elvis act.

More than a "knowing parody of a parody that doesn't know it is a parody": Andy Kaufman as Elvis in *The Midnight Special* (Sony Music Entertainment, 1981).

However, the relationship between Kaufman and Elvis Presley is not merely that of the original body of one artist to the physical simulacrum of his imitator, nor is it, as Greil Marcus argues in *Dead Elvis*, that Kaufman's Elvis act is simply a caricatured version of other Elvis imitators, and thus "a knowing parody of a parody who doesn't know it is a parody" (1999, 33). In fact, there exists an implicit alliance between Kaufman and Elvis which is much more profound than the notion of parody suggests.[9] The analogy between these two performers is probably best illustrated by reference to Elisabeth Bronfen's essay on Elvis. To begin with, when she recounts America's failure to come to terms with Presley's legendary performance on the *Milton Berle Show* in 1956, her description recalls those baffled reactions from Andy Kaufman's contemporaries who resorted to avant-gardist jargon because they did not know what to make of his performances. As Bronfen points out, though, the trouble with Elvis Presley is that his body was not simply experienced as a "scandalous" presence, but that it was always a strangely "amorphous" body as well (2002, 165). Taking this as a starting point for a cross-reading of Kaufman with Elvis, I would suggest that the same is true for Andy Kaufman.

Except for the obscene embodiment of failure that was Tony Clifton, there was nothing outrageous about the physical presence of Kaufman and his personae. What was truly irritating about Kaufman was the complete absence of any consistent personal identity that would "speak" through this body. If Kaufman's presence was scandalous, this was because the kernel of self that "inhabited" his body was so amorphous that it could never be pinpointed.

In her essay, Bronfen portrays young Elvis Presley as an entertainer who embodied a dazzling willingness to put everything at stake and be consumed by his music. This readiness to take risks, she notes, would eventually lead to the embarrassing acts of self-destruction of his later performances, and this is the point where Bronfen's analysis offers a preliminary idea of how intimately Kaufman, with his "bombing routine" and his readiness to embrace any symbolic death sentence from his audience, relates to Elvis. But, first, let me take one final detour.

Toward the end of his Kaufman biography, Bill Zehme invokes Alan Abel, a satirist and hoaxer who is probably best known for having tricked the *New York Times* into printing his own obituary on January 2, 1980, when he was in fact still alive. At first sight, this stunt seems to offer the most poignant illustration of the notion of "symbolic death" that one can imagine, as Abel, being filed under the deceased in the obituary section of a newspaper, was publicly declared dead by the letter of a social institution. Because Abel himself dispatched the letter that "killed" him, there is clearly a suicidal aspect involved in this gesture. However, this literal enactment of his self-induced symbolic death was not so radical as to oblige Abel to put everything at stake and risk his entire social existence, and this is why his fake obituary failed to constitute an *ethical act* in Lacanian terms. In fact, Zehme's account implicitly makes clear that Abel's hoax does not even qualify as a symbolic death in the strict sense of the term, because the letter that decreed his death was publicly declared invalid by Abel himself when he "called a press conference immediately after his obituary was published" (2001, 319). As Abel effectively annulled the symbolic death that he himself had induced, he revealed his gesture as a lark.

Zehme uses the anecdote of Alan Abel's premature obituary as the backdrop against which he discusses Andy Kaufman's suicidal gestures. Kaufman, he argues, understood that "Abel had not properly lingered in death. Elvis, he liked to believe, was doing it well" (319). Unlike Abel's short-lived symbolic suicide, Elvis Presley's prolonged death was such that it secured his status as an immortal cultural icon who persistently haunts America's cultural memory. After all, Presley's death still seems to foreshadow some

grand gesture of rebirth, even if this return should remain permanently deferred—and ultimately, this is precisely why Elvis is more
than just "an exemplar of the American dream," as Greil Marcus
would have it (1999, 37). As a subject that had undergone repeated
refashionings and finally succeeded in securing his own interminability, Elvis Presley embodies nothing less than the perfect trajectory as delineated by the American Dream. But if Elvis is the most
successful American Dreamer, what exactly are the implications
of Kaufman's desire "to be (like) Elvis," as it is explicitly stated at
the beginning of the documentary *I'm from Hollywood* (1989)?

In her aforementioned essay, Elisabeth Bronfen cites one of
the standard interpretations of Presley's biography, pointing out
that his career is often read "as a parable about the wonderful
promise and the terrible failure of the American Dream" (2002,
165, my translation). This is indeed one of the most popular perspectives on Elvis, but it is insufficient on several grounds, and its
crucial weakness is that it obfuscates the central inconsistency of
the American Dream as an ideological promise that necessarily
implies a dimension of tragedy even if it fulfills itself.[10] More precisely, this reading suggests that the "wonderful promise" of interminability and the "terrible failure" somehow stand in a temporal
relation with each other, the latter being the tragic outcome of the
former. Thus, this interpretation disregards the more disturbing
possibility that the immortality promised by stardom may in fact
be more intimately linked to death. Highlighting these intricacies
of death and stardom, Kaufman's performance work disclosed the
ambiguities of this supposedly sequential logic of the American
Dream.

As previously pointed out, one of the fundamental inconsistencies of the American Dream is that it obfuscates a certain
seriality of death that is inevitably an effect of its promise of
interminability. If no other figure from popular culture has ever

been as successful as Elvis Presley in terms of securing interminability, Andy Kaufman recognized Elvis as the perfect embodiment of the American Dream, because the figure of Elvis obliquely articulates the inherent paradox of the Dream that lies in these serial deaths. As Zehme reports, Kaufman "believed that there may have been four Elvises, beginning with the original, who had disappeared in 1958" (2001, 319). Clearly, this is a downright paranoid scenario on Kaufman's part, with Presley's managers in the entertainment industry figuring as the sinister authors of a conspiracy who had allegedly produced an entire series of different performers, all of which were promoted under the name of Elvis Presley.

Still, while this belief betrays the paranoia of the conspiracy theorist, its implicit logic of death and immortality as represented by the concept of stardom is completely accurate. In her essay on Elvis, Bronfen formulates this logic as follows: "We need the chosen artist who dies for us, first in a figurative sense, and then in the real, so that we can forever enjoy his transformation into the immortal, larger-than-life body of a star" (2002, 165, my translation). Kaufman's public gestures of self-immolation reveal his profound, if once again too literal understanding of this logic.

As far as Presley is concerned, Bronfen illustrates the said transformation of his body into an immortal and universally admired cultural icon by reference to the end of the film *Love Me Tender* (1956), where the protagonist played by Elvis is dead, but then his resurrection is visualized in a superimposed image of the ghostly star singing the final song: "As a 'singing corpse,' the star's body not only feeds on the substance of the real person, it also overshadows him and simultaneously proclaims the immorality of the star's image as opposed to the physical person" (161, my translation). If this visualizes the apotheosis of the immortal star, there is a strikingly analogous figure at the end of *Man on the Moon*, where Kaufman is elevated to the status of a cultural icon that will not die. In its final scene, the film re-enacts a concert performance arranged by Bob Zmuda as a way of paying homage on the first anniversary of Kaufman's death of lung cancer.

On May 16, 1985, Tony Clifton made his appearance on the stage of The Comedy Store in Los Angeles, singing Gloria Gaynor's disco anthem "I Will Survive." As this resurrection of Tony Clifton spawned speculations about Kaufman's demise, it raised the question if his death of cancer had just been the most radical version of what he would call his "bombing routine," and if Tony Clifton's posthumous appearance represented his return in the flesh, his grand gesture of rebirth, as it were. In point of fact, the man beneath Tony Clifton's excessive outfit was none other than Bob Zmuda standing in for Andy Kaufman. In the guise of Clifton, Zmuda proclaimed the immortality of Kaufman's image as a star, and there was a sense of irony about this "stand-in comedy" act that was fully in line with the way Kaufman had usually dealt with celebrity and its discontents. After all, the deceased star did not return in his own image, but dead Kaufman was resurrected in the character of his own has-been.

Fourteen years later, in the final scene in Forman's fictional biopic, this ghostly reappearance of Kaufman's Tony Clifton persona is effectively transformed into the performance of a "singing corpse" analogous to that from Elvis Presley in *Love Me Tender*. As Tony Clifton performs this song at the very end of *Man on the Moon*, the camera starts to move back, passing the faces of people who are watching what the viewer presumes is Bob Zmuda's homage to Kaufman. Eventually, though, the camera rests on Zmuda himself (played by Paul Giamatti), and this is where Forman prolongs Kaufman's endless deferral of identities in an effort to secure his interminability. After all, if Zmuda enjoys Clifton's performance in the audience, then who is the man whom we see performing as Tony Clifton onstage? As one is left to

wonder about the identity of the man who hides behind this simulacral appearance, *Man on the Moon* effectively resurrects Kaufman in the guise of Clifton, and thus visualizes the figure of the
immortal star in a way that is strikingly analogous to how Presley's
image is immortalized at the end of *Love Me Tender*.

Finally, this analogy also hints at the most fundamental difference between Andy Kaufman and Elvis Presley: In contrast to
Elvis, Kaufman's interminability was secured only belatedly, post-
actual-mortem, so to speak. To finally establish Kaufman's image
as an icon of American popular culture, the retroactive gesture of
a (moderately successful) Hollywood biopic was necessary. Andy
Kaufman, our fundamentalist American Dreamer, came nowhere
near Elvis in terms of the status of an immortal cultural icon that
marks the successfully perfected trajectory according to the ideology of the American Dream. But how can it be that Kaufman
was simultaneously more faithful to this ideological discourse,
but also less successful in terms of its promise of interminability? Implicitly, Elisabeth Bronfen provides an explanation for this
seeming paradox in her argument about the tragic dimension of
Presley's perfection of the American myth of success. The following quote provides the coordinates for my conclusion:

> If Elvis succeeded in conveying to his generation the dream that
> the impossible may become real, he did so because he transgressed
> a limit and acted against moral conventions; at the same time, he
> was necessary for the dominant system in order for it to reassert
> itself in the struggle with this force of resistance. (2002, 165, my
> translation)

In this process of absorption, the charismatic star is not only
transformed into an immortal icon, but his scandalous body is
also put at rest. However, the crucial point in this quote is that it

implicitly highlights the difference between Elvis Presley as a performer who acted against the moral codes of America, and Kaufman, who largely refrained from transgressions of any sort and did not challenge the limits of American culture. In the sense of how he relates to the American Dream, Kaufman represents Elvis Presley's uncanny sibling. As the most faithful spokesperson of the American dream-ideology, Kaufman was not absorbed by the predominant discourse, because he had always already been at the very heart of that discourse. In a way, then, Andy Kaufman was what might be called a "stand-in comedian," occupying the central void of the American Dream.

This is how Kaufman staged the uncanny center of America's social imaginary. After all, the Freudian notion of *unheimlich* designates that dimension of a subject's identity where his or her innermost kernel coincides with an absolutely foreign body. When America was confronted with this performer who embodied the uncanny kernel of its communal fantasy, the public mechanically preferred to focus on that which seemed strange about Kaufman. His performance work was read as an expression of some kind of avant-garde, and what was gladly overlooked was that Kaufman's supposed eccentricity was in fact strictly correlative to the American Dream. Hence, if the mode of overorthodoxy is more radically subversive than transgression, then Kaufman also shows that it is not necessarily more effective as a form of cultural criticism. With an ideological discourse as fluid and flexible as the American Dream, it is easy not to see that Kaufman, in his literal-minded devotion, actually staged an overconformist caricature of the Dream.

In some sense, this fundamental difference between Kaufman's obscurity and Presley's after-life as an immortal icon is mirrored in the closing scene from *Man on the Moon*. In one crucial respect, Tony Clifton's rendition of "I Will Survive" is not at all analogous to the image of Elvis Presley's singing corpse in *Love Me Tender*. The resurrection of Kaufman-as-Clifton is far more uncanny, as it exceeds the image of immortality that "feeds on the substance of the real person" in the case of Presley. At the end of *Man on the Moon*, there persists a *bodily* presence that resists dying even as the "real person" is already dead. In *Love Me Tender*, the formal device of the superimposition at the end effectively enacts the transformation of Elvis Presley's (dead) body into a *ghostly image*, a glorifying process that immortalizes his body and simultaneously puts it at rest. Strictly speaking, this kind of pacifying transformation does not take place in *Man on the Moon*, because in Forman's film we are haunted not by the image of a singing corpse, but by a *ghostly body*. To put it more succinctly, Elvis is immortalized, but Andy Kaufman is left undead.[11]

Elvis Presley's uncanny sibling: Andy Kaufman on stage in New York, 1979. From *The Real Andy Kaufman* (Eclectic DVD Distribution, 2001).

This is why the ending from *Man on the Moon* resists being read in a naively sentimental way, as a gesture that retroactively turns Kaufman into a cultural icon, securing him the status of immortality. After all, what this closing scene suggests is that Kaufman, this overorthodox subject of the American dream-ideology, renders visible the truly uncanny flipside of the glorious (if necessarily tragic) trajectory toward the immortality of stardom as epitomized by Elvis Presley, with its implication of serial deaths that must be suffered in order for the promise of immortality to fulfill itself. While Presley embodies this tragic paradox of the American Dream, then Kaufman, on his quest for interminability, ends up being undead instead of immortal. If the American Dream represents the idea of a democracy of stardom based on limitless possibilities of self-invention, Kaufman's persistent identification with this ideological discourse confronts America with the fact that any faithful enactment of this public fantasy would produce a dissipation of the self, and, consequently, lead to the death of any notion of a coherent subject.

However, the ultimate lesson of Kaufman's performance work is even more disquieting than this, and this lesson is perfectly visualized by the uncanny ending of *Man on the Moon*, as it suggests that the true horror is not the traumatic void of death. The ultimate horror is the prospect that the ideological promise of interminability as issued by the American Dream might truly fulfill itself in the flesh—not in the symbolic immortality of stardom, but in the serial subject who resists dying, as he is endlessly suspended in the space between his personae.

The interminability of Andy Kaufman is such that his body may not be put at rest, because it is totally amorphous. If Tony Clifton outlives him in *Man on the Moon*, this perfectly captures what sets Kaufman apart from Elvis, whose scandalous body is immobilized in an immortal image of stardom. Kaufman, this postmodern escape artist who took the American imperative to reinvent yourself to its literal extreme, cannot escape from being uncannily outlived by his own personae, those foreign bodies that were his own. Ultimately, this is where the American Dream reveals its fundamental inconsistency. As the ideological discourse that informs America's social imaginary and thus provides its subjects with the coordinates for their desire, the American Dream offers self-invention as a strategy that supposedly shields us from the traumatic recognition of our own mortality. The truth is, however, that this very strategy produces yet another void which is even more disturbing than that of death: the limitless void that stretches in the space of the undead.

Notes

1. Funny or Not

1. As Kaufman was just a hired actor without any authorial responsibility on *Taxi*, his appearances as Latka will not be part of this book.

2. At this stage of my argument, the notion of Andy Kaufman heading for some sort of "beyond" may seem to imply some sort of transgressive thrust. As chapter 2 will make clear, though, one of the crucial points of my argument is that Kaufman was precisely *not* a performer of transgression.

3. Here we already have one of the problems with Andy Kaufman as an object of cultural analysis, namely, that one is always uncertain as to the reliability of statements like the one cited. This dilemma is one of the central points in chapter 4.

4. In his biography of Lenny Bruce, Albert Goldman cites Bruce giving his definition of professionalism in stand-up: "A comedian should get a laugh every twenty-five seconds for a period of no less than forty-five minutes and accomplish this feat with consistency eighteen out of twenty shows" (1991, 336).

5. Strictly speaking, Kaufman's most popular persona was not Foreign Man, but Latka Gravas, who was the Foreign Man character transformed for the television sitcom *Taxi*.

6. In particular, Bill Zehme lists William K. Knoedelseder Jr., "The Identity Crisis of Andy Kaufman," *Los Angeles Times*, December 10, 1978.

7. This article is signed by one of Kaufman's own characters, his lounge-singer persona Tony Clifton. Supposedly, this was a gesture of homage on the part of the writer, who may or may not be Richard Corliss.

8. For this brief description, I am indebted to Hans Belting's chapter on the "liberation from the work of art" as featured in his extensive study *Das unsichtbare Meisterwerk* (1998, 445–52).

9. This play of cross-references recalls the attempts to integrate the subculture of punk into the cultural history of the avant-garde. Emerging in the mid-1970s, punk spanned roughly over the same period as Kaufman's career, and one of the most popular clichés about it was that it shared an affinity to the dadaist movement. However, as Greil Marcus points out in *Lipstick Traces*, there was always a curious vagueness about this kind of ready-made labeling: while punk was supposedly "like dada," he remarks, "nobody said why, let alone what that was supposed to mean" (1990, 19).

10. In what may be the first suggestion regarding Kaufman's "performance art," Phil Berger quotes Kaufman's long-term collaborator Bob Zmuda as follows: "Andy always felt he had got miscast in the comic's role. He felt that was not what he did. It was more performance art. More from the private corridors of his life. Sometimes he'd purposely go out and not try to be funny. Laughter was fine and good. But if the audience was bored, or they turned on him, that was just as good" (1985, 411).

11. Considering the video and DVD releases of Andy Kaufman's shows and television specials, it seems perfectly legitimate to pinpoint *Man on the Moon* as the key event that "recoded" Kaufman on a broader cultural scale. Nearly all Kaufman footage that is currently available was (re)released around the time when Forman's biopic premiered in 1999, or shortly thereafter.

2. The Limits of Transgression

1. Regarding the waves of political protest around the year 1968, Bill Zehme notes in his biography that at that time, Kaufman did look "like a war-protest professional, although he protested nothing, had no feelings about political unrest, had no notions toward social awareness"

(2001, 92–93). While everybody else was busy protesting, Zehme writes, Kaufman "solely concerned himself with his self-concern" (93). In a sense, this foreshadows my thesis about Kaufman's stance toward the American Dream as an ideology that is, in a curious way, all about narcissistic self-concern (see chapter 3).

2. In the videotaping of *Andy Kaufman Plays Carnegie Hall* (1979), camera angles and lighting are such that none of these images projected in the background may be discerned. I am taking this scene entirely from Zehme's account in his Kaufman biography.

3. Considering this lack of political material in Kaufman's performance work, one of his best-known self-descriptions bears a certain irony. Setting himself apart from the genre of comedy, Kaufman would call himself a "song-and-dance man," and since his own headline performances had more in common with variety shows than with "proper" comedy, the term seems fairly adequate. But then again, the same term was most famously used by Bob Dylan in 1966. In an effort to protect himself from being labeled a protest singer, Dylan referred to himself as a "song-and-dance-man," and it seems particularly ironic that someone as blatantly apolitical as Andy Kaufman should later use the exact same epithet in order to distance himself from comedy.

4. Referring to one particular act which he reads as "the essential Lenny Bruce moment," Limon points out how Bruce's threat to piss on his audience made him appear "as punishing father and naughty son in rapid oscillation, just as his audience had to vibrate . . . between terrorized child and permissive parent" (2000, 4).

5. This part of Limon's argument is largely based on Albert Goldman's detailed account of an obscenity trial against Bruce. As Goldman points out in his biography, the trial had Lenny Bruce ending up in "an oedipal nightmare" (1991, 562).

6. As quoted by Bill Zehme, though, Steve Martin himself views Kaufman's work as "a classic example of anticomedy" (2001, 198).

7. In the context of my thesis, it seems very appropriate that Kaufman should choose to read from *The Great Gatsby*, Jay Gatsby being one of the most prominent literary subjects of the American Dream. As

Jim Cullen remarks, *The Great Gatsby* has long been regarded as "the quintessential expression of the American Dream" (2003, 180).

8. The way Bob Zmuda recounts this incident in *Andy Kaufman Revealed!*, he does not make it clear if this journalist was in fact expressly hired by Zmuda and Kaufman: "Of course we had an *L.A. Times* writer named Bill Knoedelseder present," he states rather ambiguously (2001, 136).

9. Of course, this is not to play off Andy Kaufman against Lenny Bruce in terms of their subversive impact. Their respective strategies of cultural criticism are hardly comparable, since Kaufman and Bruce were operating in totally different political climates—while Bruce's aggressively open-minded stand-up confronted the paranoia of the early Cold War era, Kaufman emerged in the less repressive post-Vietnam years.

10. In his exquisite essay "A Preface to Transgression," Michel Foucault discusses this logic of transgression with reference to Bataille and Sade, insisting that transgression and the limit do not stand in a simple antonymical relationship, as does "black to white, the prohibited to the lawful, the outside to the inside." Instead, the relation between the limit and the act of transgression according to Foucault "takes the form of a spiral which no simple infraction can exhaust" (1963, 35). Yet even though such an act of transgression according to Foucault may change the symbolic field whose limit it marks internally, the problem with this "spiral" of resistance is that it is always strictly immanent, and therefore correlative, to the order it opposes.

11. The question of subversion is the subject of an ongoing theoretical debate between Žižek and Judith Butler. While Butler sides with Foucault and defends his understanding of transgression as a means of subversion, Žižek argues from a strictly Lacanian perspective and has repeatedly contested Butler's notion of subversion, most extensively so in *The Ticklish Subject* (1999, 245–312), where he offers a critical reading of Butler's *The Psychic Life of Power* (1997). Since my central thesis is mainly inspired by Žižek's writings on ideology and subversion, I refrain from further references to the theoretical rift that separates him and Judith Butler in these matters.

12. Apart from the proverbial "good soldier" Švejk, Žižek names various authors who also "subvert the ruling ideology by taking it more literally than it is ready to take itself." Referring to thinkers such as Pascal, Malebranche, Kleist, Kierkegaard, and Brecht, he argues that their writings share a structural affinity to Švejk in the sense that they display a similar kind of excessive conformism. In Žižek's words, it is precisely by way of their excessive symbolic identification that authors like these "disclose the hidden cards of the ideology they identify with . . . and thus render it inoperative—that is, unacceptable to the existing order" (1997, 77).

Interlude: The American Dream

1. In this respect, the very "idea" of America is to transcend those restrictions on personal happiness which, according to Sigmund Freud, are a necessary constituent of civilized communities. In the process of civilization, Freud writes in "Civilization and Its Discontents," "the aim of creating a unity out of the individual human beings" is far more important than the aim to secure their happiness: "It almost seems as if the creation of a great human community would be most successful if no attention had to be paid to the happiness of the individual" (1930, 140). In a way, America is all about proving Freud wrong on this account.

2. In this sense, ideology is strictly correlative to the subjective function of dreams and daydreams according to Freudian psychoanalysis. Referring to Freud's "Creative Writers and Day-Dreaming" (1908), I have already pointed out in the preface that dreams and ideologies both provide imaginary corrections of unsatisfying reality.

3. John Herzfeld's underrated media thriller *Fifteen Minutes* (2001) provides a perfect illustration of a successful ideological interpellation in Althusser's sense. In the film, two thugs from post-Communist Eastern Europe arrive in New York City, and when they are held up by the customs officer, one of them praises the films of Frank Capra and expresses his belief in America as "home of the brave." Thus, he has sufficiently proved his identity as a subject interpellated by the American Dream, and both are allowed to enter. Later, when an ad tells them to

"make your own movie," the Capra fan complies and starts to document his buddy's killing spree—thus, things go wrong when someone takes the imperative of the Dream too literally.

4. In an intriguing argument from *Disowning Knowledge*, Stanley Cavell has pointed out why the sense of tragedy is so fundamentally a part of America's history and identity as a nation. America, he argues, "is cast with uncanny perfection for its role" in tragedy, because unlike any of the other great modern nations, it was discovered; hence, America's national "fantasies are those of impotence, because it remains at the mercy of its past, because its present is continuously ridiculed by the fantastic promise of its origin and its possibility, and because it has never been assured that it will survive. Since it had a birth, it may die. It feels mortal" (1999, 115). This foreshadows my argument that at the heart of the American Dream there lies a traumatic recognition of mortality.

5. Early on in Jack Kerouac's novel *On the Road*, this ambivalence about American identities is condensed in a short passage that explicitly links the notion of self-otherness to the topography of America. This is when the narrator tells us about "the one distinct time in my life, the strangest moment of all, when I didn't know who I was . . . for about fifteen strange seconds. I wasn't scared; *I was just somebody else, some stranger,* and my whole life was a haunted life, the life of a ghost. *I was halfway across America . . .*" (1957, 19–20, my italics). Incidentally, Bill Zehme writes that Andy Kaufman used to refer to *On the Road* as if to a "prayer book, evangelically citing passages" (2001, 67).

6. In his classic *Democracy in America*, Alexis de Tocqueville already anticipated one of the fundamental ambiguities of the American "democracy of success" when he pointed out that the "very equality which allows each citizen to imagine unlimited hopes makes all of them weak as individuals. It restricts their strength on every side while offering freer scope to their longings" (1835, 624). After all, if every American subject is equally entitled to enact the myth of success, do they not actually prevent each other from success?

7. Among numerous literary illustrations of what he terms the "protean self," Lifton invokes Herman Melville's *The Confidence Man: His*

Masquerade, a novel which poses "radical questions about the capacity of people . . . to make the self over and live with more or less perpetual discontinuity and multiplicity" (1993, 42).

8. Of course, the biggest advertiser of American proteanism today is Madonna. Following the release of her latest album, *American Life* (2003), she named her traveling show the "Re-Invention World Tour," and at the end of her concerts, the injunction "Reinvent Yourself" was emblazoned on a screen covering the stage.

9. However, one should always bear in mind the paradoxical nature of the pleasure principle in the sense of a "limit to *jouissance*." According to Dylan Evans, this paradox consists in the fact that the Freudian pleasure principle prohibits "something which is already impossible; its function is therefore to sustain the neurotic illusion that enjoyment would be attainable if it were not forbidden" (2001, 92). Hence, it is the prohibition that produces the desire to transgress it for the sake of (impossible) *jouissance*.

10. The ideological interpellation of the American Dream is thus comparable to the inverted logic of repression embodied by the obscene father which Slavoj Žižek, following Michel Silvestre's concept of *Père-Jouissance*, terms "Father-Enjoyment" (1992, 125). In this sense, the American dream-ideology is analogous to the obscene father whose injunction to enjoy is what ultimately blocks the very enjoyment he explicitly commands.

11. But if you consider Dylan Evans's remark that *jouissance* is "fundamentally transgressive" (2001, 92), does this not undermine my previous insistence on the fact that Kaufman is strictly not a performer of transgression? The answer is no, because in the American Dream, it is the ideological discourse itself that functions according to the perverse logic of transgression—as for Andy Kaufman, he is merely the agent who sticks to this imperative. Within America's logic of transgression, he does not transgress its no-limits ideology, but he enacts it most faithfully, rendering visible traumatic, "lethal" *jouissance*.

12. For this point, I am indebted to Elisabeth Bronfen's rewriting of the concept of castration in *The Knotted Subject* (1998, 45–47).

3. The Postmodern Escape Artist

1. On the other hand, Kaufman's long-term collaborator Bob Zmuda points out an incident that in his opinion may be the "key that would unlock this enigma named Andy Kaufman" (Zmuda and Hansen 2001, 226). According to Zmuda, this crucial moment in Kaufman's life happened when little Andy was told by his parents that his grandfather had gone far away, while in fact he had died.

2. Of course, *Citizen Kane* already lends itself to a poststructuralist reading, because the circular structure of the film effectively deconstructs the "naive" perspective of reading "Rosebud" as the master-signifier for Kane's innermost kernel of identity. Hence, what is presented as the lost treasure of Kane's subjectivity is finally revealed to be caught up in a loop of signification where signifiers refer to nothing but (back to) themselves. The ultimate punchline, then, consists in the fact that while Alexander and Karaszewski implicitly invoke *Citizen Kane* as the paradigmatic case of the logic of "Rosebud," Welles's classic actually works very much like an "anti-Rosebud" film.

3. In his book on stand-up, John Limon argues that ultimately, stand-up comedy is always an attempt at self-escape: "All a stand-up's life feels abject to him or her, and stand-ups try to escape it by living it as an act," and as an illustration for this point, Limon refers to a portrait of comedian Ellen DeGeneres posing as human chameleon, "dressed in white and sitting in the corner of a white room, . . . trying to dissolve herself in her environment" (2000, 6).

4. Incidentally, Kaufman enjoys a clandestine cameo appearance in Ellis's fashion satire *Glamorama*. In this follow-up to *American Psycho*, the protagonists are even more vacant than Patrick Bateman, and, early on, an autobiography is mentioned that a character named Chloe has "ghostwritten with Bill Zehme" (1998, 32). As their book bears the title *The Real Me*, this is probably an ironic anticipation of Zehme's biography of Kaufman.

5. This was the first of twelve appearances Kaufman made on *Saturday Night Live* between 1975 and 1982. However, as he was never a regular member of the cast of the show, Kaufman is credited a mere footnote

in Michael Cader's illustrated history entitled *Saturday Night Live: The First Twenty Years* (1994).

6. In his biography, Bill Zehme notes that Kaufman invented this act "for little birthday children, but really for himself, when he was no more than fourteen" (2001, 152). There is a certain irony in this, because the very same act that *Saturday Night Live* producer Lorne Michaels saw as the "essence of avant-garde" (see chapter 1) was originally performance material developed by Kaufman when he was still in his early teens—at any rate, this was the legend according to Kaufman, which was reiterated not only by Zehme, but also by Bob Zmuda (Zmuda and Hansen 2001, 59) and the television documentary *Biography: Andy Kaufman* (1999).

7. On a level of trivial irony, this is true for another premiere earlier in Kaufman's career. At one of his shows at The Improvisation club in New York in 1974, a photographer from the *New York Times* took a picture of Kaufman, as yet hardly known. However, when the paper published a number of articles about the lives of stand-up comedians later that month (May 28), the caption under Kaufman's picture read "Howard Itzkowitz, a young unknown trying out at The Improvisation," as quoted by Zehme (2001, 140). Marginal as this episode may be, it reinforces the notion that Kaufman's identity was mistaken in the first place, and that his real self was deferred from the very start of his entertainment career.

8. Paul Verhoeven's underrated film *Showgirls* (1995) is arguably one of the best Hollywood pictures to show how Las Vegas functions as the phantasmatic zone where the American Dream of self-invention may be enacted for the sake of glamour and stardom.

9. This is according to Bill Zehme, who also notes that, not surprisingly, this part of the show never aired. According to Bob Zmuda's account, the incident was slightly more outrageous, with Tony Clifton "pouring the eggs over Dinah's head" (Zmuda and Hansen 2001, 173).

10. When Kaufman opened as Tony Clifton for Rodney Dangerfield at the Comedy Store in West Hollywood in 1978, he was confronted with the fact that the audience was thinking that he was the actual performer behind Clifton's make-up. According to Bill Zehme, Kaufman then admitted "that he had played Clifton before at the Comedy Store,

but this time it had been the *real* Tony Clifton onstage" (2001, 236, italics in original).

11. Incidentally, Freud's note on Falstaff in *Jokes and Their Relation to the Unconscious* offers an explanation as to why a character like Tony Clifton, as opposed to Falstaff, is not funny. According to Freud, the humorous effect of the Falstaff figure is based "on an economy in contempt and indignation. We recognize [Falstaff] as an undeserving gormandizer and swindler, but our condemnation is disarmed by a whole number of factors" (1905, 231n). In the case of Tony Clifton, the audience is not "disarmed" in any way, and there is nothing about this lousy entertainer that could seduce them into suspending their contempt for him.

12. In their notes on the shooting script for *Man on the Moon*, Scott Alexander and Larry Karaszewski point out how testimonials like these are often undermined by some process of retroactive transformation: "What's amusing is that all contemporary accounts indicate that the cast had no idea who Tony really was. But now they all wink and say they knew all along" (1999, 169).

13. For a more elaborate discussion of Andy Kaufman's career as a wrestler, see chapter 4.

14. Incidentally, this conflation evokes the tragic version of the American Dream as represented by the protagonist of F. Scott Fitzgerald's *The Great Gatsby*. As Gary Lindberg has pointed out, the character of Jay Gatsby equally shows "no distance between façade and self" (quoted in Lifton 1993, 43).

15. I borrow this pun on Judith Butler's *Bodies That Matter* (1993) from Hanjo Berressem's article entitled "Matter that Bodies" (2002).

16. Arguably, Andy Kaufman was a strictly Deleuzian performer, if there ever was one. At any rate, it might prove extremely fruitful to read his performance work in terms of the notion of "schizoanalysis" that Gilles Deleuze and Félix Guattari put forth in their controversial book *Capitalisme et Schizophrénie: L'Anti-Œdipe* (translated in English as *Anti-Oedipus: Capitalism and Schizophrenia*). According to Deleuze and Guattari, the schizo is also some sort of escape artist: "Car le schizo, ç'est celui qui échappe à toute référence œdipienne, familiale et personnologique"

(1972, 434). In this sense, Kaufman may indeed emerge as a true schizo-analyst who calls into question the postulate of personal self-identity that forms one of the primary targets of Deleuze and Guattari's critique.

17. This scene is an intricate fusion of two aspects from *The Andy Kaufman Show* (1983), and the opening sequence of *The Andy Kaufman Special* (1977). The latter begins with Foreign Man trying to persuade the audience to turn off their television sets: "There is no special, just me," Foreign Man explains, "we will just sit here for ninety minutes." *The Andy Kaufman Show* effectively annuls its own beginning by running the actual ending with final credits right at the start; toward the end of the show, the screen turns black after Kaufman is supposedly banned from television, but he makes his clandestine return in a way similar to Jim Carrey in *Man on the Moon*.

18. As Freud points out in *Jokes and Their Relation to the Unconscious*, the mode of "*mimicry*" (*Nachahmung*) offers "extraordinary pleasure" even when the objects of this imitation are not debased by the exaggeration of caricature (1905, 200, italics in original).

19. In an intriguing passage in his study *Serial Killers*, Mark Seltzer draws attention to the seemingly paradoxical logic that the very injunction to "be your self" effectively "evacuates the subject it mandates" (1998, 116).

20. Early on in his Kaufman biography, while referring to Kaufman's fascination with multiple identities, Bill Zehme invokes two characters from popular culture who serve as paradigmatic examples of the split self of American superheroes: "Superman was two guys who were one guy. Popeye ate spinach and became a different/same Popeye" (2001, 26).

21. In his article "Who's Who? Introducing Multiple Personality," Mikkel Borch-Jacobsen argues that the truly troubling question staged by the syndrome of multiple personality is "what happens when there is no 'personality', no personal identity, no 'ego' (or 'self'), no memory, no unifying pole of experience" (1994, 46). In his conclusion, he then articulates the hypothesis whether it is not precisely the "disappearance of the ego that 'multiple personality' stages in its own spectacular and derisive

fashion." After all, he asks, how "can an absence of ego be expressed, if not, paradoxically, by multiplying it?" (61). These are exactly the issues that are at stake in Andy Kaufman's performance work.

22. According to Bill Zehme, Andy Warhol sat in the front row when Kaufman played Carnegie Hall (2001, 251). Bob Zmuda, for his part, recounts that a few months before that particular show, the two met by chance in a restaurant, and Warhol invited Kaufman over to sit at his table (Zmuda and Hansen 2001, 145–46).

4. Celebrity Deathmatch

1. In his comment on Kaufman's job as a busboy, Bob Zmuda fails to see the mythological dimension of this performance, resorting to pop psychology: "Busing tables liberated him and yet at the same time secured his feet to the ground, for it was an experience completely antithetical to being a star" (Zmuda and Hansen 2001, 201).

2. The intricacies of stardom and death will be the focus of the final chapter of this book.

3. In the year 2004, the second-hand version of stardom offered by *Becoming* has developed into the more radical documentary format of MTV's *I Want a Famous Face*, which portrays people who underwent plastic surgery in order to fashion their looks according to a celebrity they adore.

4. This is one aspect where wrestling differs from boxing. In a wrestling match, there is no such thing as a "clinch" where the fight is temporarily deadlocked because the bodies of the boxers are clinging to each other. As Jan Freitag has pointed out in conversation, boxers who are interlocked in a clinch provide a perfect illustration of how Louis Althusser defines social antagonisms, namely, as a momentum of social conflict that cannot be resolved.

5. For a brief analysis of Kaufman's intergender wrestling routine in terms of gender politics, see Auslander 1992, 145–48. Referring to the openly misogynistic rhetoric of these acts, Auslander argues that it actually serves a "feminist" strategy. He also points out the ambiguities raised by the fact that Kaufman introduces the representational logic of

wrestling into the context of comedy: "Is Kaufman then *representing* a misogynistic wrestler as his comedy act, or has he *become* that wrestler? Does the comedy club recontextualize the wrestling, or vice versa?" (147, italics in original).

6. According to his profile from the *Pro-Wrestling On Line Museum*, Jerry Lawler was "arguably the biggest territorial draw in all of professional wrestling during the 1980's as he prompted sellout crowds every week, not only in his home state of Tennessee, but every where he traveled" (http://www.wrestlingmuseum.com/pages/bios/jerrylawler.html, August 31, 2004).

7. *I'm from Hollywood* (1989), a documentary film directed by Joe Orr and Kaufman's long-term partner Lynne Margulies, provides a comprehensive account of Kaufman's "conversion" from entertainer to "professional wrestler." While the film only briefly traces his "career" in intergender wrestling, it extensively documents the build-up for Kaufman's first match against wrestling champion Jerry "The King" Lawler, also covering the ensuing feud between the two.

8. On his Andy Kaufman website, B. K. Momchilow (1996) quotes the following account of the Letterman incident, issued by the World News Service on July 29, 1982: "NBC television host David Letterman sat by helplessly last night as guest Andy Kaufman and world champion wrestler Jerry Lawler turned his 'Late Night' talk show into a shambles. While Kaufman and Lawler verbally abused one another Letterman attempted to save the situation by pausing for a commercial break, at which point Lawler rose out of his chair and sent Kaufman sprawling to the floor with a ferocious blow to the face. Upon returning from the commercial break, TV viewers were treated to the sight of Kaufman spewing obscenities as censors frantically bleeped out the offensive words. Sources at NBC report that NBC officials are contemplating banning Kaufman from all future network programming" (http://andykaufman.jvlnet.com/press.htm, August 31, 2004).

9. This difference is best illustrated by referring to two performers from pop music, Eminem and Marilyn Manson. Rapper Eminem has often presented himself as the epitome of homophobic "white trash,"

thus working the social background of his biographical origins in the trailer parks of Detroit into his star persona, and in this sense, one could argue that Eminem's stance is similar to that of a stand-up comic. On the other hand, there is the bogeyman persona of shock-rocker Marilyn Manson, whose star image is devoid of any specific references to any "face" behind the excessive make-up. As a consequence, "Marilyn Manson" only exists in the artificiality of his mask—and in general, the same is true for wrestlers.

10. In what seems like the inevitable conclusion of this logic, the "Wrestling Glossary" (2004) provided by the *First Hand Wrestling* website mentions the combination of a "worked shoot," defined as an "angle that is made to look so incredibly realistic that people will think that it is actually a shoot. Often the people involved in a worked shoot will break character in order to make it look like whatever event just happened wasn't part of the script. These angles are often done to appeal to the smart fans."

11. At the time of my writing, an English translation of Pfaller's *Die Illusionen der anderen* is still in the works, to be published by Verso.

12. As I have previously argued, the exact same logic of pleasure applies to the "secondary stars" who enjoy their celebrity makeover on *Becoming*. While they clearly share an ideological distance to the idea that they might truly "become" the star they are mimicking, the important factor is that other people (such as their friends) might be duped by their performance. As in the case of wrestling, the illusion is assigned to others.

Epitaph

1. Along similar lines, Zehme also mentions Larry Cohen's feature film *God Told Me To* (1976), one of only three movie credits in Kaufman's body of work. In one brief scene of about four minutes, Kaufman makes a cameo appearance as a fake police officer who marches along with cops from the New York police force on St. Patrick's Day Parade, when he suddenly runs amok with a prop gun, before he finally drops "dead as though riddled with bullets" (2001, 157).

2. Zehme does not give full bibliographical references, but he is quoting Janet Coleman, "Don't Laugh at Andy Kaufman," *New York* magazine, September 11, 1978.

3. B. K. Momchilow (1996) offers a full transcript of Kaufman's guest appearance on Letterman's morning show, published on http://andykaufman.jvlnet.com/transdave.htm, August 31, 2004.

4. Accordingly, Bob Zmuda's version of this incident ends with his recollection of Kaufman telling him in private: "I'm dead. You happy?" (2001, 156).

5. In some sense, this scene foreshadows my final argument about the analogies that link Kaufman to Elvis Presley, because it echoes Presley's performance in his concert *Aloha from Hawaii* (1973). In her essay on Elvis, Elisabeth Bronfen argues that this concert may be read as Presley's self-conscious deconstruction of the cult he incorporates: "as if Presley, while fulfilling the wish of his fans to hear the familiar song once again, wanted to signal how much this ritual repetition bores him" (2002, 160). This reading perfectly captures what is also at stake in Kaufman's deconstruction of his popular Foreign Man persona.

6. In terms of its structure, this act recalls a brief insert from *The Andy Kaufman Show* (1983), which shows an elderly couple in front of their television set. Concerning a particular goofy scene, the man asks what it is supposed to mean, and the woman gruffly remarks, "Oh, he's playing with the medium." Thus, the self-reflexive dimension of the show is explicitly addressed, and Kaufman's "conceptualist" subversion of the medium is subverted in turn.

7. The heckling episode also made it into Forman's biopic *Man on the Moon*. In Scott Alexander and Larry Karaszewski's screenplay, the scene ends with the words "'Andy Kaufman' has been destroyed" (1999, 124).

8. In his *New York Times* review of Madonna's "Re-Invention World Tour," Kelefa Sanneh has drawn attention to this disturbing implication of any "happy version" of the serial self. Madonna, he argues, is usually imagined as a "time-lapse photograph, with one persona melting and warping into the next. It's an open-ended process, and when she's at her

brilliant best, it's easy to believe that she could keep reinventing herself forever. *But where do those old selves go?*" (2004, 1, my italics).

9. In an instance of unintentional irony, Greil Marcus points out America's awareness of Elvis Presley "as an emptied, triumphantly vague symbol of displaced identity" (1999, 33). On the same page where he dismisses Kaufman as a "sneering" parodist who fails to convey his admiration for Elvis, Marcus thus inadvertently offers a most concise summary of what Kaufman articulates in an even more radical way.

10. Another aside on Madonna: Perhaps the fact that every successful realization of the American Dream always implies a tragic dimension explains why Madonna might never be considered as true an embodiment of this Dream as Elvis Presley. As a businesswoman who is totally in control of every aspect of her star persona, she lacks the potential to become a victim of her own success in the way Elvis did. As of yet, there is simply no sense of tragedy that might come to haunt Madonna.

11. The very last frame of *Man on the Moon* shows a colorful neon sign of Andy Kaufman's head, and in a metonymic montage sequence, his image is ranked alongside the neon icons of the most classic of comedy stars: Charles Chaplin and Groucho Marx, Stan Laurel and Oliver Hardy. Still, Tony Clifton's physical presence undermines the pacifying effect of this neon sign of immortal Andy Kaufman.

Bibliography

Alexander, Scott, and Larry Karaszewski. 1999. *Man on the Moon: The Shooting Script*. New York: Newmarket Press.

Althusser, Louis. 1970. "Ideology and Ideological State Apparatuses (Notes towards an Investigation)." In *Mapping Ideology*, ed. Slavoj Žižek, 100–140. New York: Verso, 1994.

Auslander, Philip. 1992. *Presence and Resistance: Postmodernism and Cultural Politics in Contemporary American Performance*. Ann Arbor: University of Michigan Press.

Bal, Mieke. 1999. "Introduction." In *Quoting Caravaggio: Contemporary Art, Preposterous History*, 1–25. Chicago: University of Chicago Press.

Barthes, Roland. 1957. "The World of Wrestling." In Barthes, *Mythologies*, sel. and trans. Annette Lavers, 15–25. London: Vintage, 2000.

Belting, Hans. 1998. *Das unsichtbare Meisterwerk: Die modernen Mythen der Kunst*. München: Beck.

Berger, Phil. 2000. *The Last Laugh: The World of Stand-up Comics*. Updated ed. New York: Cooper Square Press.

Berressem, Hanjo. 2002. "Matter That Bodies: Gender in the Age of a Complex Materialism." In *Gender Forum* 2. http://www.genderforum.uni-koeln.de/issue.htm, August 31, 2004.

Bonitzer, Pascal. 1992. "Hitchcockian Suspense." In *Everything You Always Wanted to Know about Lacan (But Were Afraid to Ask Hitchcock)*, ed. Slavoj Žižek, 15–30. New York: Verso.

Borch-Jacobsen, Mikkel. 1994. "Who's Who? Introducing Multiple Personality." In *Supposing the Subject*, ed. Joan Copjec, 45–63. New York: Verso.

Bronfen, Elisabeth. 1998. *The Knotted Subject: Hysteria and Its Discontents*. Princeton, N.J.: Princeton University Press.

———. 2002. *"Elvis Presley*—Der Bewegte." In Bronfen and Barbara Straumann, *Diva: Eine Geschichte der Bewunderung*, 155–67. München: Schirmer/Mosel.

Butler, Judith. 1997. *The Psychic Life of Power: Theories in Subjection*. Stanford, Calif.: Stanford University Press.

———. 2000. "The Force of Fantasy." In *Feminism and Pornography*, ed. Drucilla Cornell, 487–508. Oxford Readings in Feminism. New York: Oxford University Press.

Cader, Michael, ed. 1994. *Saturday Night Live: The First Twenty Years*. Boston: Houghton Mifflin.

Cavell, Stanley. 1999. *Disowning Knowledge: In Six Plays of Shakespeare*. Cambridge: Cambridge University Press.

Clifton, Tony. 1979. "Laughter from the Toy Chest." *Time*, May 28, 78–80.

Corliss, Richard. 1981. "Comedy's Post-Funny School." *Time*, May 25, 86–87.

Cullen, Jim. 2003. *The American Dream: A Short History of an Idea That Shaped a Nation*. New York: Oxford University Press.

Deleuze, Gilles, and Félix Guattari. 1972. *Capitalisme et Schizophrénie: L'Anti-Œdipe. Nouvelle Edition Augmentée*. Paris: Les Editions de Minuit.

DeLillo, Don. 1997. *Underworld*. New York: Scribner.

de Tocqueville, Alexis. 1835. *Democracy in America and Two Essays on America*. New York: Penguin, 2003.

Dolar, Mladen. 1991. "'I Shall Be with You on Your Wedding-Night': Lacan and the Uncanny." *October* 58:5–23.

Dyer, Richard. 1998. *Stars*. New ed., with a supplementary chapter and bibliography by Paul McDonald. London: British Film Institute.

Ellis, Bret Easton. 1991. *American Psycho*. London: Picador.

————. 1998. *Glamorama*. London: Picador.

Evans, Dylan. 2001. *An Introductory Dictionary of Lacanian Psychoanalysis*. Philadelphia: Brunner-Routledge.

Foster, Hal. 1984. "For a Concept of the Political in Contemporary Art." In *Recodings: Art, Spectacle, Cultural Politics*, 139–55. New York: New Press, 1999.

————. 1996. *The Return of the Real: The Avant-Garde at the End of the Century*. Cambridge: MIT Press.

Foucault, Michel. 1963. "A Preface to Transgression." In *Language, Counter-Memory, Practice: Selected Essays and Interviews*, ed. Donald F. Bouchard, 29–52. Ithaca, N.Y.: Cornell University Press, 1977.

Freud, Sigmund. 1900. *The Interpretation of Dreams. Standard Edition*. Vols. 4 and 5, ed. James Strachey. London: Hogarth Press, 1953.

————. 1905. *Jokes and Their Relation to the Unconscious. Standard Edition*. Vol. 8, ed. James Strachey. London: Hogarth Press, 1960.

————. 1908. "Creative Writers and Day-Dreaming." In *Standard Edition*. Vol. 9, ed. James Strachey, 141–53. London: Hogarth Press, 1959.

————. 1927. "Humour." In *Standard Edition*. Vol. 21, ed. James Strachey, 159–66. London: Hogarth Press, 1961.

————. 1930. "Civilization and Its Discontents." In *Standard Edition*. Vol. 21, ed. James Strachey, 64–145. London: Hogarth Press, 1961.

Gamson, Joshua. 1994. *Claims to Fame: Celebrity in Contemporary America*. Berkeley: University of California Press.

Goldman, Albert. 1991. *Ladies and Gentlemen: Lenny Bruce!!* New York: Penguin.

James, C.L.R. 1950. *American Civilization*. Edited by Anna Grimshaw and Keith Hart. Cambridge: Blackwell, 1993.

"Kaufman, Andy." 2002. *The Internet Movie Database*. http://us.imdb.com/Name?Kaufman,+Andy, August 31, 2004.

Kerouac, Jack. 1957. *On the Road*. New York: Penguin, 1972.

Kosuth, Joseph. 1969. "Art after Philosophy." In *Conceptual Art: A Critical Anthology*, ed. Alexander Alberro and Blake Stimson, 158–77. Cambridge: MIT Press, 1999.

Kristeva, Julia. 1982. *Powers of Horror: An Essay on Abjection*. New York: Columbia University Press.

Lacan, Jacques. 1997. *The Ethics of Psychoanalysis, 1959–1960. The Seminar of Jacques Lacan, Book VII.* Edited by Jacques-Alain Miller. Translated by Dennis Porter. New York: W. W. Norton.

Laplanche, Jean, and Jean-Bertrand Pontalis. 1964. "Fantasy and the Origins of Sexuality." In *Formations of Fantasy*, ed. Victor Burgin, James Donald, and Cora Kaplan, 5–34. New York: Routledge, 1989.

"Lawler, Jerry." 2002. In *Pro-Wrestling On Line Museum*. http://www. wrestlingmuseum.com/pages/bios/jerrylawler.html, August 31, 2004.

Lifton, Robert Jay. 1993. *The Protean Self: Human Resilience in an Age of Fragmentation*. Chicago: University of Chicago Press, 1999.

Limon, John. 2000. *Stand-up Comedy in Theory, or, Abjection in America*. Durham, N.C.: Duke University Press.

Marc, David. 1989. *Comic Visions: Television Comedy and American Culture*. Boston: Unwin Hyman.

Marcus, Greil. 1990. *Lipstick Traces: A Secret History of the Twentieth Century*. Cambridge: Harvard University Press.

———. 1999. *Dead Elvis: A Chronicle of a Cultural Obsession*. Cambridge: Harvard University Press.

McDonald, Paul. 1998. "Reconceptualising Stardom." In Dyer, *Stars*, 175–200. London: British Film Institute.

Momchilov, B. K. 1996. *Goofing on Elvis. The Andy Kaufman Homepage*. http://andykaufman.jvlnet.com/toc.htm, August 31, 2004.

Nash, Michael. 1990. "Andy Kaufman's Last Laugh." Pre-publication draft. *Art Issues* 10. http://www.concentric.net/~Mnash/text/essays/kaufman.html, February 27, 2002.

Ohrt, Roberto. 1990. *Phantom Avantgarde: Eine Geschichte der Situationistischen Internationale und der modernen Kunst*. Hamburg: Edition Nautilus.

Pfaller, Robert. 2002. *Die Illusionen der anderen: Über das Lustprinzip in der Kultur*. Frankfurt a.M.: Suhrkamp.

Pfaller, Robert, ed. 2000. *Interpassivität: Studien über delegiertes Genießen*. New York: Springer.

Rich, Frank. 1999. "American Pseudo." *New York Times Magazine* (Section 6), December 12, 80–114.

Rifkin, Jeremy. 2004. *The European Dream: How Europe's Vision of the Future Is Quietly Eclipsing the American Dream*. New York: Jeremy P. Tarcher.

Salecl, Renata. 1994. *The Spoils of Freedom: Psychoanalysis and Feminism after the Fall of Socialism*. New York: Routledge.

Sanneh, Kelefa. 2004. "Madonna's Latest Self, a Mix of Her Old Ones." *New York Times* (Section E), May 26.

Seltzer, Mark. 1998. *Serial Killers: Death and Life in America's Wound Culture*. New York: Routledge.

"Wrestling Glossary" 2000. In *Pro-Wrestling On Line Museum*. http://www.wrestlingmuseum.com/homeie.html, August 31, 2004.

"Wrestling Glossary." 2004. In *First Hand Wrestling Website*. http://fhwrestling.com/glossary.php, August 31, 2004.

Zehme, Bill. 2001. *Lost in the Funhouse: The Life and Mind of Andy Kaufman*. New York: Delta.

Žižek, Slavoj. 1992. *Enjoy Your Symptom! Jacques Lacan in Hollywood and Out*. New York: Routledge.

———. 1994. "The Spectre of Ideology (Introduction)." In *Mapping Ideology*, ed. Žižek, 1–33. New York: Verso.

———. 1997. *The Plague of Fantasies*. New York: Verso.

———. 1999. *The Ticklish Subject: The Absent Centre of Political Ontology*. New York: Verso.

———. 2000. "Die Substitution zwischen Interaktivität und Interpassivität." In *Interpassivität: Studien über delegiertes Genießen*, ed. Robert Pfaller, 13–32. New York: Springer.

Zmuda, Bob, and Matthew Scott Hansen. 2001. *Andy Kaufman Revealed! Best Friend Tells All*. Boston: Back Bay Books.

Filmography

Andy Kaufman Film Footage

Andy Kaufman Plays Carnegie Hall. [1979] 2000. Dir. Julian Goldberg. Perf. Andy Kaufman. Paramount Pictures.

The Andy Kaufman Show. [1983] 2000. PBS Soundstage Series. Dir. Dick Carter. Perf. Andy Kaufman. Rhino Video.

The Andy Kaufman Special [Andy's Funhouse]. [1977] 1998. Dir. Tom Trbovich. Perf. Andy Kaufman. Anchor Bay.

Biography: Andy Kaufman. 1999. Dir. Lynne Margulies and Bob Zmuda. Narrated by Danny DeVito. A&E Television Networks.

I'm from Hollywood. [1989] 2000. Dir. Lynne Margulies, Joe Orr. Perf. Andy Kaufman, Jerry Lawler. Rhino Video.

The Midnight Special. [1981] 2000. Dir. Tom Trbovich. Perf. Andy Kaufman. Sony Music Entertainment.

The Real Andy Kaufman. [1979] 2001. Dir. Seth Schultz. Perf. Andy Kaufman. Eclectic DVD Distribution.

Other Films

Funny Bones. 1995. Screenplay by Peter Chelsom and Peter Flannery. Dir. Peter Chelsom. Perf. Oliver Platt, Jerry Lewis, and Lee Evans. Hollywood Pictures.

Man on the Moon. 1999. Screenplay by Scott Alexander and Larry Karaszewski. Dir. Milos Forman. Perf. Jim Carrey, Danny DeVito, Courtney Love, and Paul Giamatti. Universal Pictures.

Zelig. 1983. Screenplay by Woody Allen. Dir. Woody Allen. Perf. Woody Allen, Mia Farrow, and John Buckwalter. Orion Pictures.

Index

Florian Keller is a writer and fellow at the Institute of Cultural Studies in Art, Media, and Design at the School of Art and Design, University of Applied Sciences and Arts, Zürich, Switzerland.